Leading With Character, Purpose, & Passion!

A Model for Successful Leadership at Work and Home

Roger M. Weis, Ed.D.
Vernon W. Gantt, Ph.D.

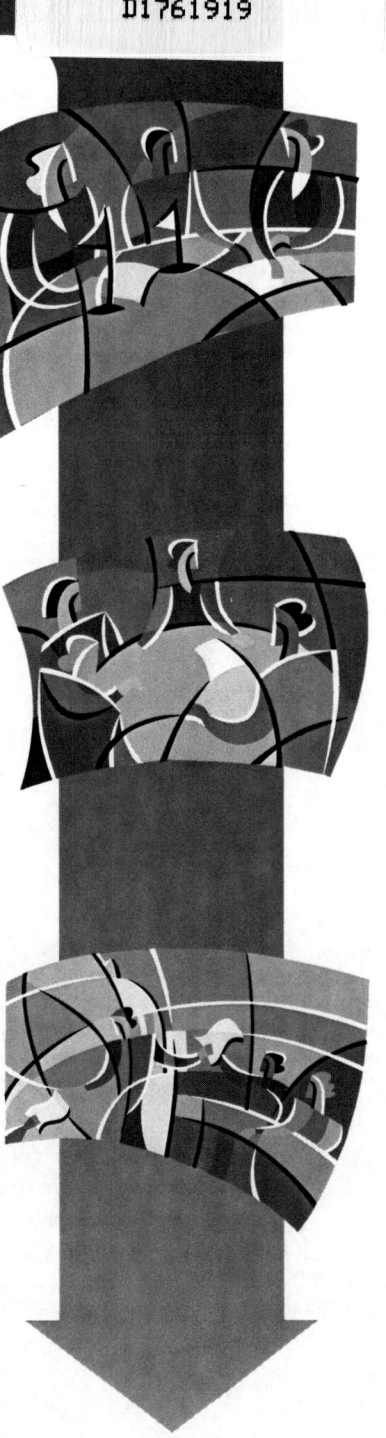

KENDALL/HUNT PUBLISHING COMPANY
4050 Westmark Drive   Dubuque, Iowa 52002

Ordering Information:

Address: Kendall/Hunt Publishing Company
4050 Westmark Drive, P.O. Box 1480
Dubuque, IA 52001-1840

Phone: 800-228.0810

Fax: 800-772-9165

Website: www.kendallhunt.com

Copyright © 2009 by Kendall/Hunt Publishing Company

ISBN 978-0-7575-5746-0

All rights reserved. No part of this publication may be reproduced, stored in a retrieval system, or transmitted, in any form or by any means, electronic, mechanical, photocopying, recording, or otherwise, without the prior written permission of the copyright owner.

Printed in the United States of America
10 9 8 7 6 5 4 3 2 1

DEDICATION

I dedicate this book to the many friends, family members, and colleagues who have shared so much of their love and support with me over the years and who have been instrumental in making the world a much better place for everyone; and I thank God for the many blessings He has provided me with.

—Roger M. Weis

I dedicate my portion of this book to Emma C. Gantt. I now understand why grandparents can be so proud. I pray for her to have a life filled with people of character, purpose, and passion.

—Vernon W. Gantt

CONTENTS

Acknowledgments vii

Introduction ix

PART I Combining Character, Purpose, & Passion With Leadership 1

PART II Leading With Character, Purpose, & Passion at Work & at Home . . .31

Epilogue 153

Bibliography 155

About the Authors 161

Leadership Development Workshops and Seminars 163

ACKNOWLEDGMENTS

The authors acknowledge and thank a number of people for their guidance on the journey to understanding, teaching, and writing about leadership. They include Dr. Christopher R. Edginton for his encouragement in the development of our first textbook, which included a chapter on leadership. It would also include Dr. Fenwick English, a great teacher and authority on leadership himself, who shared his thoughts and beliefs with many, and Dr. Gary Brockway, who leads everyday with character, purpose, and passion. We also thank Dr. Robert F. Long of the W. K. Kellogg Foundation for his support of our earlier research and publications, along with Jerome and Jeanette Cohen for their kindness and generosity toward earlier works.

Special thanks goes to our research coordinator Dr. Steve Cox for his efforts in locating excellent resources; to research assistant Robin Esau for her expertise and dedication to this work; and to Cooper Levering and Linda Pierce for their assistance with graphic arts.

We also express our appreciation to those closest to us, our family members Stefani Weis, Clint Weis, Annika Weis, and Riley Weis, and Dolores (Dee) Gantt, Michelle Gantt, Darren Gantt, Lindy Gantt, Emma Gantt, and Virginia Gantt for their never-ending support and encouragement.

A percentage of the profits from each book will go toward supporting charitable organizations.

INTRODUCTION

Each year, a number of books are written about leadership concepts, and many are written with great insight and quality. The unique insight this book offers is developed from years and years of researching, teaching, and practicing leadership concepts, and then pulling that experience into a focused vision. This vision, if effectively understood, could make an unparalleled difference in your life at home and at work.

We are not offering a magical pill or even a step-by-step process. What we offer is the opportunity for you to first understand leadership and the importance of concepts such as character, purpose, and passion within the realm of leadership. Then, you will learn how to apply this realization to make a positive difference in all of your relationships and interactions. Many authors and experts within the leadership field concentrate on developing a step-by-step process on becoming a strong leader. While this method does have its advantages, it is important to first realize that *character* is the backbone of a person. An individual with good *character* is naturally respected, trusted, and followed. When this same person has a clearly defined sense of *purpose* and demonstrates a genuine *passion* for that purpose, this individual can make a demonstrable difference in the people he or she comes in contact with every day.

While character, purpose, and passion are vital in leadership, it is also important for an individual to have *competencies* in various skill areas or know how to collaborate with individuals with similar or different competencies to make a difference in the lives of others.

An individual who integrates character, purpose, and passion into his or her leadership style and who has developed competency areas is an individual who will be trusted and sought after. In the Revised Integrated Leadership and Character model (Figure 2, p. 33), the leadership attributes of character, purpose, and passion are incorporated with three different yet interrelated competency areas to produce exciting and long-lasting results when understood and used appropriately. In the original model (Figure 1), purpose and passion were considered to be parts of character (Weis and Gantt, 2004).

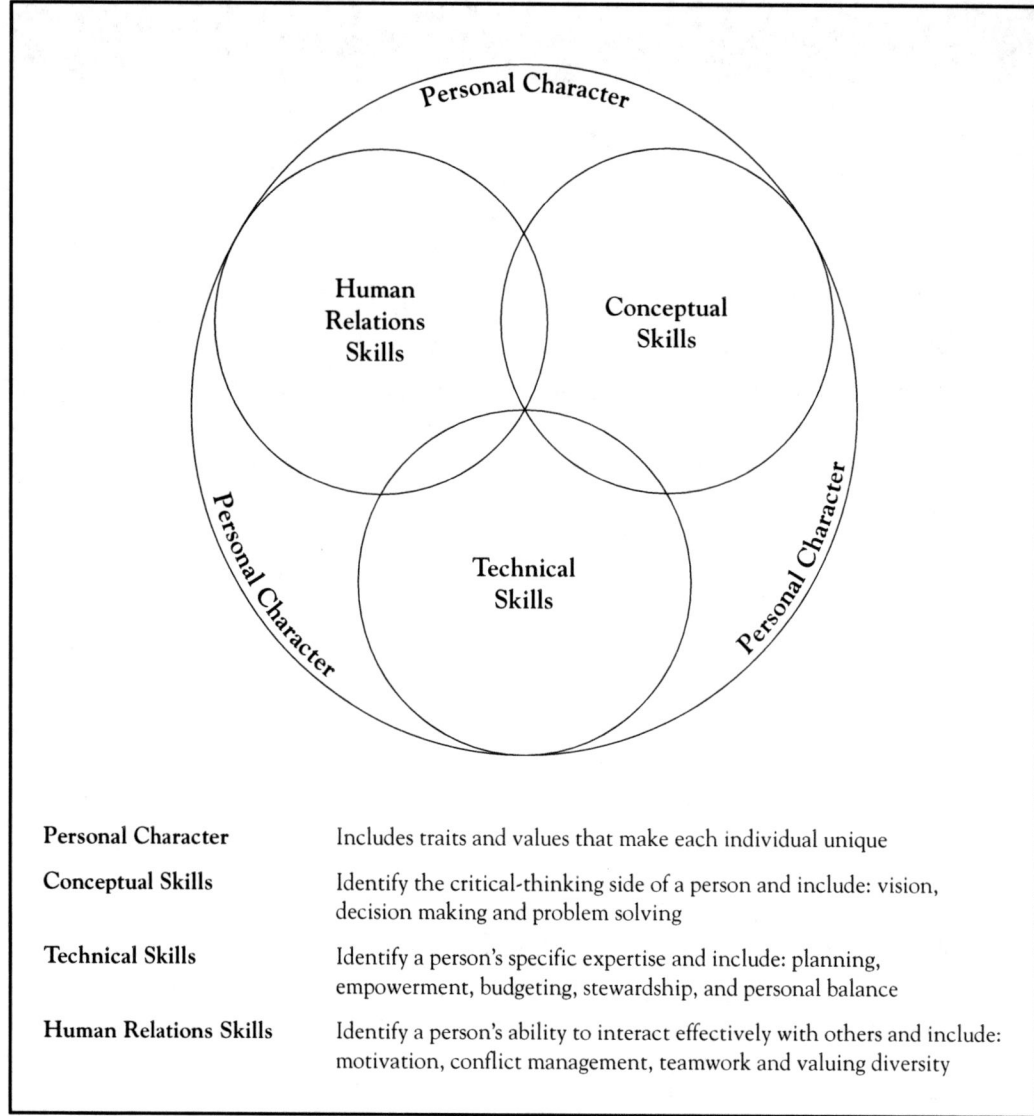

Personal Character	Includes traits and values that make each individual unique
Conceptual Skills	Identify the critical-thinking side of a person and include: vision, decision making and problem solving
Technical Skills	Identify a person's specific expertise and include: planning, empowerment, budgeting, stewardship, and personal balance
Human Relations Skills	Identify a person's ability to interact effectively with others and include: motivation, conflict management, teamwork and valuing diversity

FIGURE 1 Integrated Leadership and Character: Original Model
SOURCE: Roger M. Weis and Vernon W. Gantt

Part I of the book explains the essence of leadership and how important it is in the success of groups, whether at home or at work. It lists the four ways individuals can develop as leaders: (1) studying leadership theories, (2) critiquing the lives of leaders, (3) being mentored by a leader, and (4) learning leadership through experiential activities, with specific examples of all four areas before introducing the revised Integrated Leadership and Character Model. Part II of the book describes the revised model in more detail including the importance of character, purpose and passion and the significance of the interrelated competency areas; conceptual skills, technical skills, and human relation skills in the overall success of a leader at home and at work.

PART I

Combining Character, Purpose, & Passion With Leadership

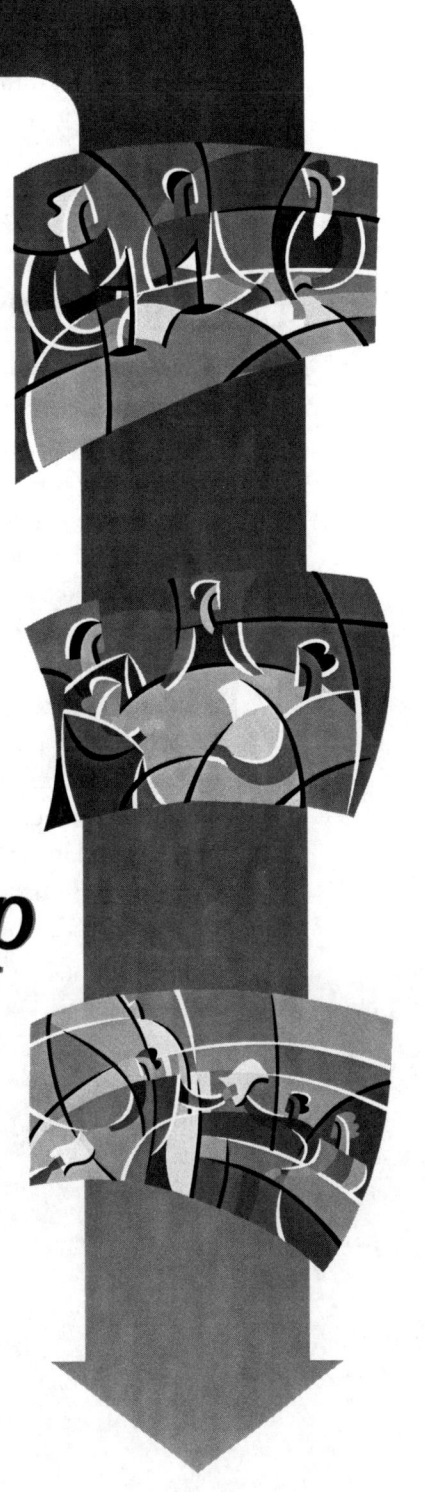

Because it is vital to the survival of families, communities, businesses, organizations, and even nations, thousands upon thousands of books and articles have been written on the subject of leadership. But what really is leadership anyway, and how important is it at home and at work?

The Essence of Leadership

There are almost as many definitions of leadership as there are authors and other experts who describe it. We offer a simple, operational definition of leadership that incorporates the important aspects of other definitions and works well with our forthcoming discussions: *Leadership is about inspiring, guiding, and influencing others to reach goals and make a difference* (Weis and Gantt 2004). It is about recognizing there is a need—in a family, community, or organization—and accepting the risks involved (and there are almost always risks) in leading others from point A to point B in order to reach hopeful outcomes.

Strong leaders are *inspiring*. They recognize needs and issues that must be addressed, and they are excited and committed to resolving or managing those challenges. Leaders not only share that recognition with others, but they also encourage others to offer their ideas and suggestions. This is a concept referred to as *shared vision*. Group members in a family or an organization are more likely to buy into the process to address various needs if they have had the opportunity to offer input into the way these issues should be addressed and also feel that their input was well received. And, when group members share the vision and understand the process of reaching that vision, an unparalleled synergy develops toward addressing the issues and reaching the goals.

> *If your actions inspire others to dream more,*
> *learn more, do more and become more,*
> *you are a leader.*
>
> —John Quincy Adams

Successful leaders offer competent *guidance* by first developing a shared vision, and then organizing a process to reach the goals effectively and harmoniously. They realize the importance of each individual in reaching group goals, and they work hard to *empower* others by providing ideas, training, support, and encouragement, which results in a base of *empowerment*. Individuals who are empowered can operate with confidence and competence, and feel encouraged to rely more and more on their own initiative. When individuals are encouraged to operate with a degree of autonomy and freedom, they acquire a high degree of self efficacy and believe their efforts are making a difference (Bennis and Townsend, 1995).

Finally, and perhaps most importantly, good leaders understand how vital it is to use their *influence* to motivate and encourage group members to perform at the highest levels. In fact, many authors equate leadership with influence, which is the ability to affect the attitude and behavior of others through the relationship. Leadership is often defined as the ability to develop followers who will work with the leader to reach their goals (Maxwell, 1993). And one of the most important pieces in that developmental process is having influence so that others will commit to the group's goals and to the processes involved in reaching those goals.

> **The key to successful leadership today is influence, not authority.**
> —Kenneth Blanchard

Because influence is so valuable to leadership, it is important to discuss the various ways that individuals develop influence over others. One significant way to develop influence over others is through the use of *power*. People sometimes think of power as a negative thing, but when equated with influence, power is one of the most desirable traits that a leader can have. In a seminal study, French and Raven (1968) identified six sources from which power can emanate—referent power, legitimate power, expert power, reward power, coercive power, and information or persuasive power—and these sources of power could be used individually or in combination. Let's look at the significance of each source of these sources of power in the context of influence.

Individuals often become leaders because they are perceived as having energy and charisma (*referent power*). Leaders with referent power have influence primarily through their personality and likeability, and often develop a strong and loyal following from group members.

Others develop a foundation of power primarily through the position or office that they hold (*legitimate power*). People who influence others through an official position can be very persuasive and the authority that goes along with an office can be significant, particularly in hierarchical organizations.

A strong source of influence includes individuals with specific knowledge and skills in particular areas (*expert power*). These individuals are often in high demand and their leadership level is primarily based on the successes they have experienced.

Individuals who offer rewards for desirable behavior can be very influential (*reward power*). The rewards can be either tangible or intangible in nature and, in a work environment, can include salaries, bonuses, and promotions, as well as other appropriate forms of appreciation.

Leaders can also use the threat of punishment to move things along effectively (*coercive power*). This power is particularly important in areas of accomplishing goals and in policies that have to do with safety and health issues in families and in organizations. Coercive power must be applied to the correct level and used skillfully to avoid distrust, hostility, and turmoil.

In making decisions on activities, services, or products, families and other organizations are often faced with difficult decisions. A leader with accurate and up-to-date information can more easily guide the group toward effective decisions (*information* or *persuasive power*).

Reflection & Application

Because influence and power are so important, we ask you to take a few minutes and complete the following activities.

First, consider a supervisor you have had in the recent past; then list his/her sources of power in order of priority. How successful was this person with this profile?

_____

_____

Now associate each source of power with a former United States president.

1. Referent _____

2. Expert _____

3. Legitimate _____

4. Reward _____

5. Coercive _____

6. Persuasive _____

How effective was each president in using a particular source of power?

1. _____

2. _____

3. _____

4. _____

5. _____

6. _____

Next, list your own sources of power in order of priority and consider how successful you are when using each source.

1. _____
2. _____
3. _____
4. _____
5. _____
6. _____

Finally, rent or purchase the movie *Dave*. Watch from when Dave meets the little boy in the homeless shelter, to the scene where Dave's security guard interrupts his wife in a meeting (approximately 14 minutes). Can you identify how each of the six sources of power was used during this period in the movie?

1. Referent _____
2. Expert _____
3. Legitimate _____
4. Reward _____
5. Coercive _____
6. Persuasive _____

These activities are great to share with colleagues or family members. Spend time discussing any differences in your perceptions of power and its use.

How Do Leaders Differ from Managers?

Being aware of our bases of powers is important, and being able to effectively incorporate these sources of power to influence others in accomplishing goals can lead to great successes at work and home.

A long-standing discussion on the differences between leaders and managers exist. *Managers* are usually considered individuals with an official position who direct, control, and organize tasks and individuals, whereas *leaders* are individuals who recognize needs and are willing to take risks in inspiring, guiding, and influencing others to address needs and issues in order to make a difference. Leaders don't necessarily need an official position to be effective. Leaders and managers are important for different reasons. Both *delegate* to others by providing individuals with opportunities to share in responsibilities and authority. Responsibility and authority must be shared in a family and any organization for the group to succeed. Good leaders and managers then monitor the progress of group members and make adjustments when necessary, a process often called *responsible delegation*. A number of experts believe that families and other organizations should try to develop *leader-managers* (Hitt, 1988) these individuals who know how to organize and direct and also have the ability to inspire individuals to high levels of accomplishment primarily through the relationship.

It is our fervent belief that good leaders are made not born. If knowledge and skills can be developed, then individuals can acquire the characteristics and skills that are necessary to inspire, guide, and influence others to address needs and meet goals. Many people just want to succeed without necessarily "leading" the way, so why should one want to become a good leader in a family or an organization? The fact is, if you equate leadership with influence, which most experts in the field of leadership do, then you have no choice but to become the best leader you can possibly be! Each of us wants to have an influence with our family, with people at work, and with our friends and other community members. We need to become the best leader we can, for their well being and for ours.

> Begin where you are
> and do what you can.
> —Arthur Ashe

Leadership Development from Within

Thomas Cronin, former White House Fellow, stated that leadership cannot be taught, as such, but that each individual must learn in their own minds the strengths and limitations of leadership (Wren, 1995). There are four proven ways to develop as a leader:

- Study leadership theories and models
- Assess the actual lives of leaders for understanding/inspiration
- Ask to be mentored by leaders in your field of interest
- Learn to be a leader through experiential activities and practice

Each of these areas has significance in the overall development of leaders in families and organizations, so let's take a brief look at each.

> To be a great person, walk hand-in-hand and side-by-side with great people.
> —Nido Qubein

Leadership Theories and Models

One way to become a better leader is through the study of leadership theories and models and there are many to consider. We have selected five models that all include character as an essential ingredient and that correlate in some respects with the Revised Integrated Leadership and Character Model (Figure 2, p. 33) that we present later in the book. These five models have been selected for their value to you as a developing leader. Each is reviewed in brief.

Transformational Leadership. In 1978, Burns suggested that it was possible for individuals to motivate each other toward higher levels of satisfaction and stated that *transformational leadership* occurs "when one or more persons engage with others in such a way that leaders and followers raise one another to higher levels of motivation and morality" (Burns, 1978, p. 20).

Transformational leadership is a leadership process based on fairness and trust: A leader assumes that individuals need commitment and self-fulfillment, then empowers and inspires individuals to work together to achieve greater and greater goals. Burns said that "transformational leadership was elevating, and can take place in many aspects of our personal and professional lives" (Burns, 1978, p. 455). Peters and Waterman (1982) supported Burns, stating that transformational leadership is a great way to inspire individuals, (families), and organizations in the pursuit of excellence. The same authors noted that individuals will commit a great deal of themselves to efforts they perceive as worthwhile. A good transformational leader gets involved with others and works closely with individuals in the group—side by side whenever possible—in the shared desire to make a difference in a family, organization, or community.

> Great leaders have a high regard for achievement, and an even higher regard for people!
> —Roger M. Weis

Principle Theory. The idea of leaders incorporating virtues, values, or principles in their leadership style has been thought about, written about, and practiced for centuries and is now generally referred to as the *principle theory*. Plato and Aristotle emphasized that leaders should place less emphasis on rules and focus more on developing good habits such as justice, prudence, courage and temperance, which were then considered virtues. Later, Christian writers added virtues such as treating others equally to this list, making virtues qualities with both earthly and heavenly rewards. Virtues are considered qualities that, when followed, allow us to reach "good goals" and to refrain from temptations and distractions (MacIntyre, 1981).

Many now consider virtues to be values or the principles that guide our lives. Character traits such as honesty and patience have often been mentioned as critical parts of effective leadership. In the 1980s and 1990s, Stephen Covey (1989) expanded the idea that effective living and leadership could only be achieved if individuals integrated principles such as *integrity, honesty, service,* and *excellence* in their daily activities. He stated that people could maintain these principles by developing certain habits, or purposeful systems of maintaining principles in all that we do. Leading with principles can result in strong and trusting relationships. Stephen Covey's book, *The 7 Habits of Highly Effective People* (1989) is a wonderful resource for leading with principles and is recommended by the authors.

Collaborative Leadership. A more contemporary style of leadership, *collaborative leadership*, involves bringing people together to build trust, cooperation, and communication. The concept emphasizes sharing ideas and listening, understanding, and often acting on the input of those involved. Eisler (1995) stated that collaborative leaders avoid dominating and directing approaches and develop a nurturing environment of support and trust. Group members are treated as important and worthwhile individuals.

In the book *The Flight of the Buffalo*, Belasco and Stayer (1993) discuss how collaborative leadership also involves taking turns at leading, depending on the circumstances and situations. They describe good leaders as those who empower others to lead under specific conditions and who don't feel threatened by others taking a leadership position. The same authors make an interesting comparison of collaborative leadership and geese; geese communicate continually during flight and take turns leading when one becomes tired or the situation changes in some way. In *collaborative leadership*, effective communication and trust are encouraged, as is the sharing of leadership. Individuals are encouraged to accept positions of leadership when it is appropriate and helpful for the goals of the group.

Invitational Leadership. In the book *Becoming an Invitational Leader: A New Approach to Professionalism and Personal Success*, Purkey and Siegel (2003) develop a holistic and dynamic model of leadership suggesting that leaders need to "invite" their colleagues, family members, and others to participate in happier, more effective relationships. They suggest that leaders practice four specific values or guiding principles when "inviting" others to participate in more successful processes and activities; these are *respect, trust, optimism,* and *intentionality*.

A very important aspect of leadership is letting others know that we value them, and one of the most important ways to do this is by acting *respectful* of others, by being courteous, and by expressing appreciation and care. The importance of respect should come into play on a day-to-day basis and is extremely important during times of crisis. By *trusting* others we're letting them know that we trust their abilities and their integrity. Trust is created when families and organizations share a set of values; although there is a certain level of vulnerability attached to trust, there is a greater strength in trusting relationships. *Optimists* tend to expect the very best from the human spirit and often work diligently to turn negatives into positives. Optimists believe that each individual, family, and organization can and should be striving toward full potential. Good leaders are optimists.

Intentionality is a key part of the invitational leadership concept because such leaders intentionally focus on being respectful, trustworthy, and optimistic. This focus encourages individuals, families, and organizations to be the very best they can be and to grow stronger together.

Servant Leadership. Robert K. Greenleaf is credited with a theory of leadership in which an individual begins with a natural feeling of wanting to serve others first. That individual then makes a conscious decision to develop as a leader. Greenleaf designates this theory as *servant leadership*, a concept he developed after reading Hermann Hesse's *Journey to the East* (Greenleaf, 1970). In this book, a group of men are on a mythical journey and are sustained by their servant, Leo, who provides various tasks for the group while maintaining their spirits with his optimism and joyful nature. All goes well on the journey until Leo disappears and the group and their journey fall into disarray for a time. Years later it is learned that Leo was actually a noble leader who sponsored the journey in the first place.

According to Greenleaf, a *servant-leader's* passion is to make sure that people's needs are being served and they are growing stronger and more competent and confident as the servant-leader works to empower them. A servant-leader works for his or her people and does everything possible to help them accomplish goals and be successful. A good servant-leader places the well being of others above him/herself and often directs credit for successes to others.

> It is high time the ideal of success be replaced by the ideal of service.
> —Albert Einstein

Each of the above models is an excellent demonstration of the importance of principles and character in the leadership process involving families and organizations. We will come back to some of these models later in this book.

Reflection & Application

There are many, many other important leadership models and theories. Discuss with your co-workers who in your organization practices each one of these theories. How do they act? What do they do that identifies them with the theory you've chosen for their leadership style?

1. Transformational _____
2. Principle _____
3. Collaborative _____
4. Invitational _____
5. Servant _____

Ask family members about people past or present who live up to the leadership style descriptions provided in these pages. Why were or are those people considered examples of the theory?

1. Transformational _____
2. Principle _____
3. Collaborative _____
4. Invitational _____
5. Servant _____

Once you learn the stories of current or past leaders, share them with new members of your work team.

Are there other leadership models you are familiar with and fond of?

What do you like about the model(s)?

Is character an important aspect of the model(s)? If not, could/should character be integrated in the model(s)?

Assessing the Lives of Leaders Past

Another great way to learn and develop as a leader is to assess the actual lives of leaders. This can provide a strong base of understanding and inspiration for self development. We can learn from both the successes as well as the failures of past leaders.

According to *Lao Tzu,* a Chinese philosopher who lived in sixth century B.C., leaders should place the well being of others above themselves, and should serve more as a facilitator rather than a task maker (Wren, 1995). He believed that leaders should be nurturing, caring, and interested in the individuals being led and that credit for success should be directed toward others. He also believed that when a leader felt it necessary to take a stronger leadership stance in certain circumstances, group members should still feel as if they were being assisted rather than led, so they could maintain a sense of autonomy. It is easy to see that Lao-Tzu was an *empowering* individual and that his type of leadership led to mutual trust, motivation, and empowerment for those involved.

Thomas Jefferson was born into a prominent Virginia family in 1743; his father was a wealthy plantation owner and his mother was from distinguished Scottish and English families (Koch and Peden, 1993). He was the primary author of the Declaration of Independence, the founder of the University of Virginia, and the third president of this country. He was brilliant as a statesman, scientist, inventor, educator, and even architect. His vast knowledge and statesmanlike abilities assisted him greatly in moving the country forward and toward independence from England. His southern, aristocratic culture, however, led to a contradiction. The same man who wrote, "We hold these truths to be self-evident, that all men are created equal, that they are endowed by their Creator with certain unalienable Rights, that among these are Life, Liberty, and the pursuit of Happiness" in the Declaration of Independence continued to buy and sell slaves, and did so even as president. Jefferson will always be remembered as one of the greatest leaders of the country, but he will also be remembered as a man of significant paradox.

Harriett Tubman grew up as a slave on the eastern shore of Maryland in the early 1800s and learned early in her life how it felt to be oppressed and devalued (Petry, 1955). As a young girl, she had to work in the fields of the plantation where she lived from dusk to dawn and was often hired out to other families for cleaning, weaving, and caring for children. When she became a young woman, Tubman was determined not to live life as a slave and made the decision to run away toward the North even though her husband John refused to accompany her. Her escape was assisted by the Underground Railroad, which was little more than a loosely organized group of people who provided shelter and food for the travels ahead. Tubman made it safely to freedom in the North, but she kept returning to the South again and again to lead other slaves to freedom despite the overwhelming danger. Harriett Tubman led with compassion, conviction, and determination.

> The woods are dark and deep,
> but I have promises to keep,
> and miles to go before I sleep,
> and miles to go before I sleep.
>
> —Robert Frost

Clara Barton was born on Christmas day in 1821 and grew up in Oxford, Massachusetts; she was rather shy as a youngster (Boylson, 1955). As a young adult, she became a teacher and was admired by her students for her caring ways and determination to be involved with their lives even out of the classroom. When war broke out between the states, Barton worked as a nurse, saving countless lives, often working from daybreak to past dusk. Later, while visiting in Europe, she learned about the International Red Cross (IRC), an organization that provided relief efforts for individuals during times of upheaval. When she returned, she began organizing the American version of the IRC to provide relief services for victims of disaster. She was soon appointed to be president of the National Red Cross, which later became the American Red Cross. Her caring nature, vision, and determination would change the shape of a nation and the lives of millions of people for decades to come.

George A. Custer was a graduate of West Point and first served as a general in the Civil War. He was considered a hero by many for leading troops against the Confederate cavalry and defending the Union army from Confederate infantrymen (Utley, 1998). His superiors described him as a warrior who fought with courage, conviction, and an unparalleled fury and focus on victory. As a matter of fact, had it not been for a place in Montana called Little Big Horn, he could well have become President Custer because of his competencies and determination.

After the Civil War, Custer was sent by his government to protect pioneering Americans as they moved West. He became famous for his successes fighting the Indians, but Little Big Horn came to be his undoing when he faced an enemy enraged by past atrocities. Overconfident from past successes, Custer underestimated the strength of his enemy and overestimated his own competencies and the will of his troops. Custer and all of the men in his unit were lost.

As a youngster in Tuscumbia, Alabama in the early 1900s, *Helen Keller* lived a fairly normal childhood until she reached the age of nineteen months when a high fever left her both deaf and blind (Richards, 1968). With limited capabilities for healthy communication, she became something of a behavior problem until she was introduced to Anne Sullivan. Sullivan herself had almost become blind and overcame many obstacles to become a teacher of the blind, the deaf, and the mute. Because of Sullivan's skills and determination, Keller began to read and write using Braille and grew calmer as her communication opportunities increased. Eventually, Keller mastered four different types of alphabets and wrote her own story about growing up with so many challenges. The story became a book, *The Story of My Life*, which was printed in 50 different languages. Keller went on to encourage thousands of others with similar afflictions and was deeply involved with the American Foundation for the Blind. She also wrote *Teacher* as a tribute to her teacher and mentor, Anne Sullivan. By using compassion, love, and skill, Anne Sullivan and Helen Keller worked together to overcome extraordinary circumstances and their work changed the lives of thousands of others.

> **The most beautiful things in the world cannot be seen or even touched. They must be felt with the heart.**
>
> —Helen Keller

Ask almost any migrant farm worker to name his hero and he will often answer emphatically with the name *Cesar Chavez* (Levy, 1975). Chavez grew up in the town of Gila Bend, Arizona, where his family owned land and businesses. But the depression of 1929 left them virtually penniless and they had to leave their home and revert to a life of picking crops. The conditions in the labor camps where the Chavez family was forced to live were often horrible with no electricity, heat, or running water. The school system the Chavez children attended was considered racist and children were actually punished for speaking Spanish. Later in life and following a stint in the U.S. Navy, Chavez took a position with the Community Service Organization where he registered people to vote and learned about power, organizing agencies, and initiating sit-ins. He carried these attributes with him when he organized the National Farm Workers Association to successfully work for decent wages and benefits for ordinary farm workers. In spite of working in opposition to the powerful California Growers Association, the Teamsters Union, and the AFL-CIO, Chavez maintained nonviolent strategies to win fairness for farm workers. Chavez employed organizational skills, determination and a commitment to the common good to overcome seemingly insurmountable obstacles.

It is important to assess other leaders to determine the kinds of character traits and areas of expertise that appeal to us. The leaders discussed here had high levels of character and various areas of expertise and, for the most part, they successfully incorporated their character and expertise for the common good. In some instances, however, we can see where a flaw in character or a lack in skill can lead to failure. When we see admirable character and skills in others, we should strive to emulate those areas in ourselves. When we see flaws in their character and skills, we try to avoid those deficiencies. We can learn from their successes and from their failures.

There are thousands and thousands of "leaders" we have come to respect and admire. Some of them are in the next room or down the street or across town; they are a part of our families and our social circles. Others are written about and discussed locally, nationally, and beyond.

List some leaders who are especially important to you.

What do you admire about them?

What have you learned from them? Explain each example.

_____
_____
_____
_____
_____
_____
_____

How important was character in your selection of each leader?

_____
_____
_____
_____
_____
_____
_____

How can these people help you be a better leader at work, at home?

_____
_____
_____
_____
_____
_____
_____

Mentoring and Leadership

Another way that we can all develop our leadership abilities is through the process of *mentoring*. Individuals can become more successful at home or at work by being supported and helped by others more experienced than they. A mentor can provide direct guidance and support as well as offer suggestions regarding outside resources such as training opportunities, workshops, seminars, and even counseling or coaching. Successful mentoring can only take place in the context of a trusting relationship. Individuals involved in mentoring must engage in a genuine communication process characterized by good interaction, a problem-solution mindset, an attempt to develop new ideas, and a collaborative thought process (Bokeno and Gantt, 2000).

There are four key components in a good mentoring relationship: *caring, sharing, correcting,* and *connecting* (Gantt, 1997). Mentoring is not an assignment; it defines a relationship and only works when individuals develop a genuine trust for each other and *care* about the well being of the other person. Concern for another individual can be demonstrated in part by *sharing* information or strategies that can be beneficial in different types of situations. Another important component of mentoring is *correcting* another person when they are behaving or thinking in negative, dysfunctional, irrational, or self-defeating ways. This is the trickiest of the four key components because it can sometimes be interpreted as criticism and must be implemented carefully and skillfully. Finally, a good mentoring relationship includes *connecting* individuals to others who also may be helpful in their growth as a people and as leaders.

> The greatest good you can do for another is not just to share your riches but to reveal to him his own.
>
> —Benjamin Disraeli

Reflection & Application

Almost all of us have been coached, empowered, and mentored by others.

Who comes to mind when you think of someone who has spent a good deal of time offering you guidance and support?

_____
_____
_____
_____
_____
_____
_____
_____

What were some of the most helpful suggestions they made to you?

_____
_____
_____
_____
_____
_____
_____
_____

What can/should you do to be a better mentor for others?

_____

_____

_____

_____

_____

_____

_____

What benefits have you personally recognized from being mentored at work or at home?

_____

_____

_____

_____

_____

_____

_____

Learning to be a Leader Experientially and through Practice

Another way for individuals to develop as leaders is participation in activities that provide opportunities for skill and character development through *experiential learning* processes. This is considered by many to be one of the strongest ways to learn about various content areas by incorporating that knowledge through practical experience activities. Businesses, nonprofit organizations, and educational institutions often provide internships or student teaching opportunities. Individuals can take what they have learned in classrooms, seminars, and workshops and, with the help of experienced supervisors, modify that knowledge to fit the needs of the organization. One of the fastest growing pedagogies in educational institutions and service organizations is *service learning*. Service learning is field experience that combines community service with various learning objectives (Weis and Gantt, 2002). Studies indicate that individuals make significant strides in areas of personal growth, career development, social development, and cognitive development through service learning activities.

> I hear and I forget.
> I see and I remember.
> I do and I understand.
>
> —Confucius

Families should be and often are involved with experiential learning activities. A father may provide coaching for his daughter in the knowledge and skills of a sport, for instance, then support further practice and involvement in a team sport. A mother may teach her son the importance of respect and service then get involved with him in serving meals at a local homeless shelter. Whether experiential learning takes place in a home, a business, or another setting, it is very important that instruction of the content area is delivered effectively, and that the experiences are supported and monitored effectively as well.

Finally, it is important to remember that we need to practice, monitor, and adjust the leadership concepts we have learned continuously until they are most effective for us. And once they are effective, we need to practice, monitor, and adjust again and again. Leadership development only stops when you let it stop!

Reflection & Application

Think about some experiential learning situations you have been involved with recently or in the past.

What are some of the lessons you have learned or are learning from those experiences?

_____
_____
_____
_____
_____
_____
_____
_____

Will you be able to use these lessons in the future toward being a better leader? How so?

_____
_____
_____
_____
_____
_____
_____
_____

PART II

Leading With Character, Purpose, & Passion at Work & at Home

The Revised Integrated Leadership and Character Model (Figure 2) was developed as a framework for including the three leadership attributes mentioned earlier in one concept. When understood and applied, it can make an unparalleled difference in how we lead and influence those around us (Weis and Gantt, 2004). It is an assessment and development tool for self improvement, as well as an assessment and development concept for families and organizations, and it has been used nationally and internationally in the selection and training of staff members in various organizations. As well, it has been included in textbooks and journals nationally and internationally. The model was developed through a three-year research project involving hundreds of individuals, community leaders, and educators.

According to the model:

- To be successful, leaders must have the kind of personal character (traits and values), sense of purpose, and level of passion that is important in leading a family or organization successfully.

- Additionally, they must possess or develop appropriate levels of conceptual, technical, and human relations skills (Katz, 1955), or be able to collaborate with those who possess them.

- The interaction and effectiveness of the three skill and knowledge areas or competencies are dependent on the character, purpose, and passion of the leader.

In the original model (Figure 1, p. x), purpose and passion were subsumed within or understood to be a part of character, but each of these aspects is extremely important. Therefore, the revised model includes these areas in a deservedly prominent role. Next, we'll look at how the model might play out at work or at home.

To develop effective products or services in any organization, a leader must have a sense of what the customers, clients, or members need and want (*conceptual skills*). He or she must be able to follow-up on this vision with competent skills in planning and implementing products, programs, or services (*technical skills*), and must be able to effectively explain and motivate personnel in creating products or services and constituents to buy products or participate in programs or services (*human relation skills*). When good leaders are not well versed in competency areas, they are skilled in collaborating with those who are. The more trusted, focused, and determined an individual is to make the product or program work (*character, purpose,* and *passion*) the more likely the product or program will succeed. The same process should work for any activity in any organization (Weis, Rogers, and Broughton, 2006).

PART II Leading With Character, Purpose, & Passion at Work & at Home

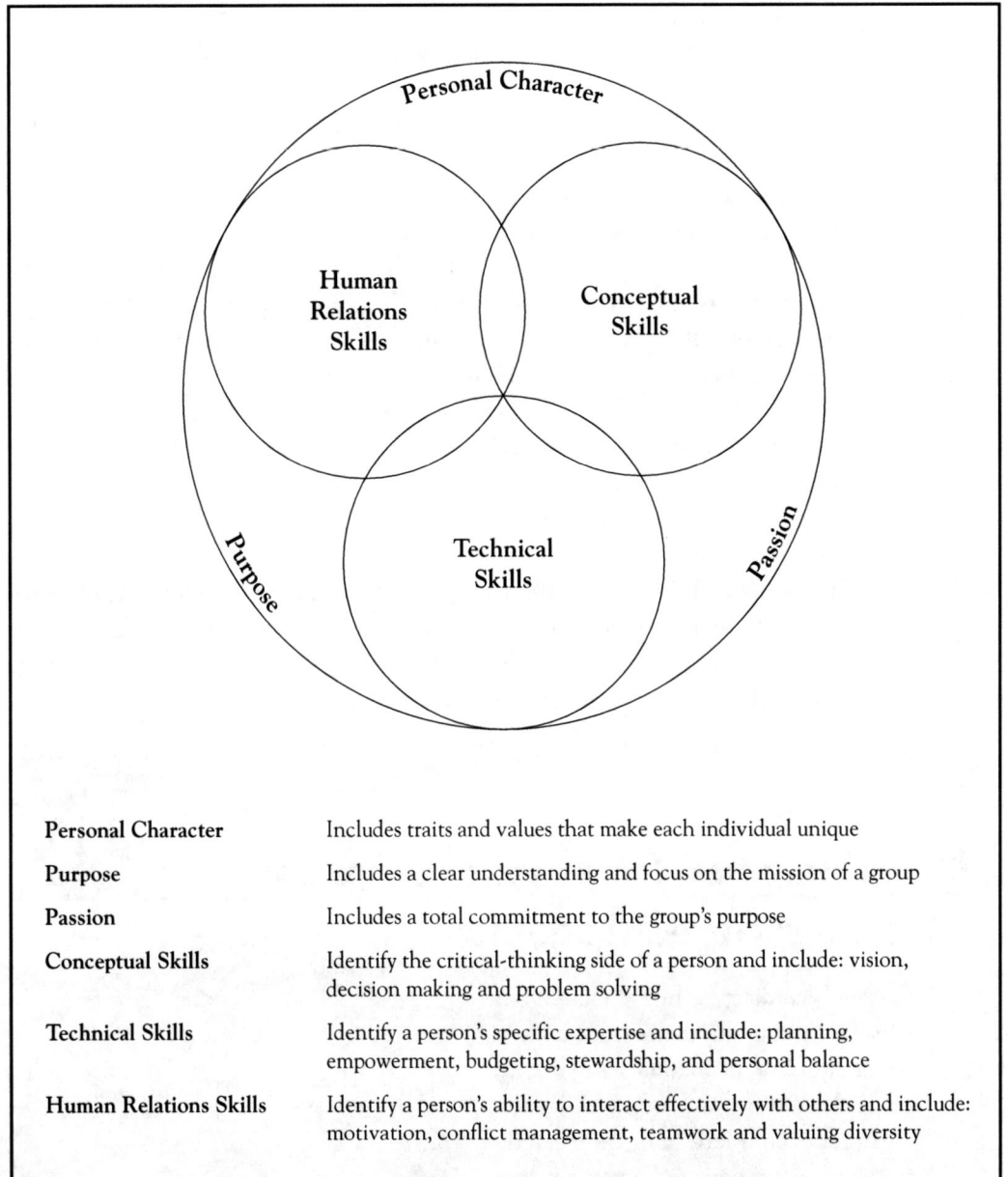

Personal Character	Includes traits and values that make each individual unique
Purpose	Includes a clear understanding and focus on the mission of a group
Passion	Includes a total commitment to the group's purpose
Conceptual Skills	Identify the critical-thinking side of a person and include: vision, decision making and problem solving
Technical Skills	Identify a person's specific expertise and include: planning, empowerment, budgeting, stewardship, and personal balance
Human Relations Skills	Identify a person's ability to interact effectively with others and include: motivation, conflict management, teamwork and valuing diversity

FIGURE 2 Integrated Leadership and Character: Revised Model
SOURCE: Roger M. Weis and Vernon W. Gantt

This same concept works in a similar way in a family setting. Family leaders must learn what family members need and want (*conceptual skills*). They must be able to develop processes in which family members can reach their goals (*technical skills*), and they must be able to communicate and motivate family members toward their needs (*human relations skills*). The more respected, focused, and determined the leader (*character, purpose,* and *passion*), the more likely family members will be to buy into the process for achieving family goals together.

Now that you have been introduced to the model, we will amplify the individual components and explain how they link character, purpose, and passion at home and at work. If you wish to have any influence on family members, organizational constituents, or community members, becoming a leader is a requirement, not an option. Being the best leader possible takes planning, thought, and determination. Becoming a successful leader at home and at work is the overall goal of the Integrated Leadership and Character Model, which provides a structure for self assessment and development for individuals in both settings. It can also be used for assessing and developing others.

In the rest of Part II, we will attempt to explain the three main leadership attributes of the model in more detail, interrelate competency areas that are important in making a difference with others, and integrate the model in the contexts of home and work, beginning with the leadership attributes.

How Character, Purpose, and Passion Hold the Model Together

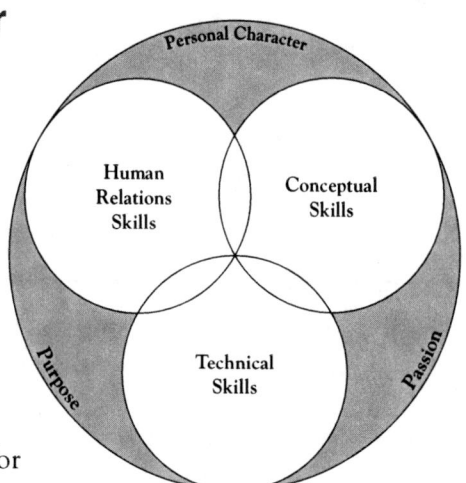

Personal character is the essence of who a person is and includes the traits and values that define individuals and distinguish them from each other. A leader with good character can be trusted, respected, and counted on to get the job done effectively within the framework of the shared values of other group members. Additionally, leaders must focus on the group's shared vision or *purpose*, and have an absolute *passion* for that purpose. Although the three interrelated skill areas shown in Figure 2 are critical to the success of any group, the interaction and effectiveness of those competency areas are dependent on the character, purpose, and passion of group leaders and of other members of the group.

The Importance of Character, Purpose, and Passion in Leading

Within the context of leadership, personal character, purpose, and passion are each important in their own way. Leaders with good character are respected and often followed. Good leaders help group members maintain a focus on the purpose of the family or organization, and often demonstrate an immeasurable passion for that purpose, which can be contagious for other group members. Although these three attributes are interrelated, just as with the three competency areas, we'll look at each separately in the next section.

Personal Character as a Critical Aspect in Leadership

The role that character plays in leadership cannot be overstated. *Personal character* includes the traits and values an individual chooses and develops to govern his or her life. It is not an accident; we choose the traits and values we deem important. An individual with the greatest of skills and competencies can fail miserably if there are significant chinks in their character—this has been proven again and again throughout history. Although no one is expected to be perfect, leaders must choose a direction in life that will enable them to lead effectively and enable others along the way. First, we'll look at the traits and values we believe are essential for effective character, then we'll discuss ways to develop character.

Traits and Values Critical for Good Character

There are as many lists of important traits and values for character as there are experts and authors. Traits are those characteristics that make us unique; values are the principles that guide our lives. The following is a select list of traits and values, blended from various experts and references, that we believe are essential for strong character. These references include the "Six Pillars of Character" from *Character Counts* (Character Counts, 2007), a list of attributes important for leadership endorsed by 17,000 individuals from 62 countries from the GLOBE Study (House, et al., 2004), a selection of character traits from leadership authors John Maxwell, (Maxwell, 1999) and Stephen Covey (Covey, 1989), suggested attributes on character from the book, *The Leadership Challenge*, (Kouzes and Posner, 2002) and our own list from the textbook *Knowledge & Skill Development in Nonprofit Organizations* (2004). Although not intended to be all inclusive, we believe these traits and values are absolutely necessary for successful leadership at home and at work.

Traits and Values to Ensure Good Character

1. **Commitment.** One of the most important attributes that leaders must have is a very strong commitment to the mission of the group and to individual group members. As long as the mission of the group is clear and encompassing, then all activities can be designed toward that mission, and it is the group leader's responsibility to ensure that group members remain focused on their mission. (The importance of mission or *purpose* will be discussed separately and in detail later on in the book.) It is also critical that group leaders frequently communicate—verbally and by their actions—their commitment to the success and well being of each and every member of the group. Commitment on the part of leaders of a group is crucial and adds a high level of legitimacy to the purpose of the family or organization.

2. **Integrity.** One of the strongest characteristics necessary for good leadership is integrity. This means that group members and others will be able to trust a leader to be honest, responsible, and effective in helping his or her group reach their goals. Integrity inspires confidence from others, and it is so much easier for groups to be successful when leadership has a proven track record for being trusted and dependable. Integrity also assumes that leaders will be fair and treat each individual with respect.

As we mentioned earlier, no one is expected to be perfect; if and when a leader errs in the area of integrity it is crucial to correct that mistake quickly, genuinely, and appropriately and to learn from any such error.

> *Leadership is a combination of strategy and character. If you must be without one, be without the strategy.*
>
> —Gen. H. Norman Schwarzkopf

3. **Concern.** Leaders who express genuine concern for group members and others associated with a group's mission help them feel cared for and important, and make it much easier for them to work toward the purpose of the group. Expressing a real interest in the lives of others demonstrates that individuals are just as important as the mission of the group, and helps members feel a real sense of belonging. It also helps to strengthen the bonds between leaders and group members.

4. **Competence.** Competencies in conceptual, technical, and human relations skills are the nuts and bolts of a successful group, and leaders should be aware of these areas for themselves and for other members of their group. Competencies can be developed or learned; individual group members can and should work together in improving or enhancing various skill areas to help reach the goals. Being an expert in all three areas in the context of various situations is extremely difficult if not impossible. Instead, good leaders must know how to blend the skills of team members, when to train those who need to further develop skill areas, and how to collaborate with others to bring expertise into the group as necessary.

5. **Communication.** Effective communication means providing an environment in which individuals can more freely express their ideas, needs, and concerns. The environment needs to be safe, encouraging, and receptive to new and even unusual directions that might help the group to grow and be successful. It is important for group members to feel comfortable to express his or her thoughts clearly and often if necessary.

Effective leaders try to listen and understand group member's communication and take action when it seems right to do so. Leaders can also use communication as a tool for encouragement and motivation.

6. **Determination.** Each day of our lives includes hurdles and obstacles to overcome, it seems. Successful leaders work well with others to develop methods to address issues and to move past situations that impede progress toward the group's goals. Good leaders are not easily swayed in the presence of what may seem like overwhelming odds, and work hard, patiently, and diligently at finding just the right solution to potential pitfalls. It is important too that leaders help group members stay together as a team and maintain a confident attitude while addressing problems. Groups that succeed over and over again in the face of adversity are strengthened by the experiences and are more and more willing to take on challenges when they know there is a genuine resolve to be successful.

> Always make a total effort, even when the odds are against you.
> —Arnold Palmer

7. **Flexibility.** Because there are so many complexities involved in leading a family and an organization, leaders must be able to effectively coordinate numerous activities at the same time. Good leaders recognize the many different dimensions involved in any group and are able and willing to coordinate the resources available to enable that group toward success in many different areas often at or around the same time. They must be able to adjust well to change and, in some instances, initiate change (Weis and Gantt, 2004). And they must be able to wear a number of different "hats" with different situations and different individuals and relationships. We once had a graduate who took a position as program coordinator for a youth and human service organization. He compiled a list of 25 "roles" he had taken on in his new position; they included: counselor, coach, teacher, nurse, negotiator, custodian, accountant, and policeman among others. Successful groups require a leader who can serve with flexibility

8. **Courage.** British Prime Minister Winston Churchill thought that courage was the most esteemed human quality "because it is the quality which guarantees all others." Leadership is about taking risks to make a difference, and courage is the willingness to take those risks in order to make improvements or to initiate a new activity, service, or product. Courage is inspirational, and group members who sense that their leader is willing to take a chance to make a difference are more likely to take risks as well. If you were to speak with successful business or sports leaders about failure, they would say that they did a lot of things that didn't work or struck out a number of times, but they had the courage to try something again and again until it worked more often than not. Courage is also about remaining true to a principle in spite of the difficulty; this helps make courage contagious for others in a group.

> Life has its own hidden forces which you can only discover by living.
> —Soren Kierkegaard

9. **Win/Win Approach.** Leaders should try to approach each situation, conflict or activity with the sense that everyone will benefit from what is about to transpire. In his book *The 7 Habits of Highly Effective People*, Stephen Covey's Habit No. 4 was "Think win/win." He realized that everyone involved in a situation would feel much more comfortable with decisions and directions if they were mutually beneficial. They therefore would be more supportive of action plans designed around those decisions and goals (1989). When there is a win/win culture in any family or organization, members feel a stronger connection to the group and are often more committed to the overall purpose and goals. Leaders must create an environment that rewards actions and outcomes that are mutually beneficial. The win/win approach is an important concept and will be discussed again in a later section.

10. **Citizenship.** One of the most important values for any group is that they work together to make their community and the world a better place.

Activities within the group can include adopting a nonprofit organization to support and/or discussing issues and current events to help individuals decide their position to take action such as in voting or volunteering. Working together can make constructive changes in a community while building camaraderie among group members. Group leaders should also encourage individuals to take part in organizations outside the group on their own, such as with service organizations, religious institutions, and other civic minded associations.

Reflection & Application

There are many other resources lists other character traits and values, but we believe the 10 we included are critical for a leader to succeed within his or her family or organization.

Take some time to look over the list of personal character traits and values. Which of these traits and values to you believe you are strong in?

Although I find all traits & values important, I feel communication is imperative to all relationships. Commitment & determination are also high on my list

Which do you need to work on?

Courage - When placed in problem situations, I tend to back down. Courage would prove useful in head-to-head situations.

Are there other traits and values you believe must be included as part of such a list? What are they and why do you believe they should be included?

_____
_____
_____
_____
_____
_____
_____

PART II *Leading With Character, Purpose, & Passion at Work & at Home*

Creating an Environment for Effective Character Development

Emphasizing good character at work and at home can improve morale while it increases the effectiveness of the group. Next we want to look at ways to develop good character in yourself and others because, just like leadership or competency areas, character is something that can be developed through a healthy and focused environment.

> Good character is more to be praised than outstanding talent. Most talents are, to some extent, a gift. Good character, by contrast, is not given to us. We have to build it piece by piece—by thought, choice, courage and determination.
>
> —John Luther

Creating an environment that enriches the development of good character takes a great deal of time, thought, and commitment but it is crucial for the well being of individuals in the group and of the group's overall well being and success. The following steps toward developing a healthy environment for good character are best achieved when addressed in the sequence suggested below.

▸ *Assessment and Commitment.* Family and organizational leaders need to study the list of character traits and values that were compiled earlier. Check with other group leaders and members and see what they think about the list and make changes as deemed necessary. It's important that this is a *shared vision* of traits and values for individuals to buy into the list more readily. Try and keep the list to between 10 and 15 areas at most. Once you've completed this, then you should assess yourself against the list of traits and values you have identified as critical for good character. Most of us will usually feel strong in some areas and understand that we need to work harder in others. Make the commitment to do just that; work harder to be fully committed to the traits and values that you and your group have deemed necessary and even critical for success. Remember, actions speak louder than words. Live your life committed to your group and its values. Express yourself with integrity and determination. Let group members know you genuinely care about them. Groups with leaders of strong character have a much easier time of developing good character for themselves.

- *Preparing Others for Character Enrichment.* Once the list of traits and values is established and the leaders are determined to follow the guidelines of specific traits and values, then it's time to share the list with others. Group members need to understand why these traits and values are essential for success before they will be accepted and followed. Formal and informal meetings can begin to take place with leaders explaining how important these kinds of traits and values are and how they should be incorporated into the fabric of the group. Change is not always easy and often takes courage, determination, and patience before results can be appreciated.

- *Encourage Others Toward Success.* As we mention above, change is not easy especially if it involves a significant difference in the way something has been done in the past. We all get into routines and habits but we need to break out of those routines and form new habits if we want to improve. Rewarding others for their commitment and belief in the traits and values the group has selected is important for change to occur. Praise, pats on the back, and celebrations of all kinds should be considered for individuals and teams who demonstrate strong character.

- *Model Good Character.* Unfortunately, there are a number of "leaders" who too often adopt the old adage "do as I say not as I do." No one expects any member of a group to follow traits and values exactly, but it is very important that group leaders make every attempt to live their lives within the parameters of the traits and values the group has decided upon for good character. It may place an added burden on leadership but it is a burden that is well worth the effort. It is much easier for group members to immerse themselves in the guidelines of good character when they see family and organizational leaders leading the way. And it takes practice, lots and lots of practice, to do what's clearly right over and over again.

♦ *Review and Amend the Character Development Process as Needed.* Like any process in a family or organization, the process of character development should be reviewed from time to time to be certain that individuals continue to understand the importance of remaining true to the traits and values that the group has adopted. Leaders and members may be having a more difficult time adapting to particular traits and values and if those remain important to the group, then discussions should be planned around those difficulties. Also, other traits and valued may need to be added from time to time if the review process suggests additions. Just like the original list, it is much easier to buy into a new list if each person has some say so in the decision making process.

Just as character is the backbone of an individual, it can and should also be the backbone of what a family or organization stands for; character development for individuals and groups is critical for the foundation of any and all success. Leading with character means leading with the traits and values that you genuinely believe in and that will make a positive difference in the lives of many.

While character is critical for success it is also important to have a clear *purpose* for any family or organization and a strong *passion* for that purpose. Next we'll look at the importance purpose plays in the success of a group.

Purpose Provides a Clear Direction for Success

Character is very important for the success of any group; it is equally important that group members have a clear direction for their actions. While most businesses and other organizations have a mission statement or statement of purpose, most families usually have an unwritten, understood but sometimes unclear mission. And even organizations with existing statements of purpose can review those statements for clarity and improvement.

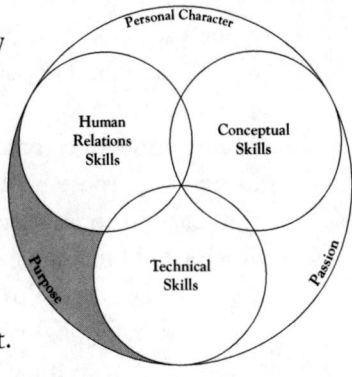

A clear and strong purpose for any organization is like a beacon of light that helps to guide, govern, and inspire group members toward the goals of the organization (Covey, 1991). Understanding the purpose of a group and feeling like an integral part of that purpose makes all the difference in the world. Group members who feel they are an important part of the purpose, stay focused toward the purpose and have much higher morale and commitment to the family or organization.

A purpose or mission statement is a vision of what a group hopes to achieve. It should include the overall goals that the group is striving to accomplish, as well as some of the core values like the ones discussed a little earlier in this book. Including goals and values in a statement of purpose allows the group to strive for what they hope to accomplish while maintaining the values they have set for themselves. For a business, the mission statement might include something about creating the highest quality products while maintaining great customer service. Another part of the statement of purpose could mention the importance of teamwork, open communication, and integrity in the development of high quality products. Yet another part of a statement of purpose could include the organization's commitment to the professional development of each employee and to civic responsibilities through financial and volunteer opportunities. Youth and human service organizations such as Rotary International, the Lions Clubs, Boys and Girls Clubs of America, NAACP, YMCA, and Women's Clubs also include their goals and values with their statement of purpose. If you go to the home page of almost any business or organization, you'll usually find their purpose statement on the very first page.

For a family, the statement of purpose should also concentrate on the values and goals on which the family is focused. Caring and commitment for one another and for members of the community, the importance of integrity, trust, love, and communication, and the promise to help each family member become the best person he or she can become are all important considerations for a family's statement of purpose.

A statement of purpose should be broad enough to encompass important goals and values and so it is not limiting in its scope. At the same time, it needs to be specific enough so that individuals have a clear understanding of what the group's mission or purpose is all about.

Leaders in any organization should strive for a *shared purpose* for their group, which would include getting as much input from group members as possible. For a statement of purpose that will be valued by everyone, everyone in the group should express their thoughts. Providing opportunities for individuals to freely express their thoughts on the purpose statement allows group members to get to know each other better and appreciate each other more. The statement of purpose needs to be shared with prospective new employees or new members of a group, so that the prospective members can decide if they are comfortable with the group's purpose. A purpose statement should be inclusive but brief so that it is easy to remember and becomes part of one's identity. Purpose statements can be several sentences, a paragraph or two, and even a page or two but usually no longer than that. This provides significant space to be inclusive but keeps it brief enough to be effective.

Staying *focused* on the mission of a group is not easy; there are lots of distractions and hurdles to overcome while maintaining focus. The following is a list of steps for leaders to use as a reference when helping group members stay focused on the purpose of their family and/or organizations.

Steps to Stay Focused

- *Develop a Shared and Effective Statement of Purpose.* Some of the best organizations in the world are where they are today because they asked their members and customers (for businesses) for input on the content of the purpose statement. Getting input from all those concerned can provide valuable information, while allowing group members to feel like an important part of the group. After requesting input from those involved, set times for discussions of the various ideas. Make drafts of the proposed statement of purpose and share them with all those involved.

    Before preparing a final draft, be sure you include all the people who are a part of the organization and the constituents involved, and the goals and values of the group. Make sure the statement is comprehensive enough to cover the most important aspects of the mission, specific enough to be clearly understood, yet brief enough to be easily followed. A good purpose statement is something that individuals will be attracted to, will believe in, and will feel fortunate to be a part of.

- *Share Your Purpose.* Once a statement of purpose is completed, it must be communicated to anyone associated with your organization, concentrating first on group members and then anyone else associated with your group that you feel needs to know about your purpose. This varies considerably, of course, depending on whether your group is a business, another kind of organization, or a family. A summarized version of your purpose statement can be written on letterheads, posted throughout the home, business, or organization. It can be posted on a web site—many families and most other types of organizations have web sites these days. Good organizations require individuals to go through organizational training; be certain that the training involves understanding of the purpose statement and how important the purpose statement is to the success of the group. Continue emphasizing the message in the purpose statement through various meetings and activities.

♦ *Reinforce Members for Incorporating the Group's Purpose.* Members who make the purpose of the group a significant part of their culture should be acknowledged and reinforced for living with the goals and values of the organization, and making those goal and values as special as they should be. Pats on the back, verbal praise, dinners out, awards, bonuses, raises, higher allowances, group celebrations—these are all things that leaders can and should consider to emphasize the importance of living with the culture established by the statement of purpose. Just following an organizational purpose that you genuinely believe in can be motivating in and of itself.

♦ *Model Your Purpose.* Just like other areas of leadership, when leaders model the purpose and are closely aligned with the values and goals associated with the purpose statement, it adds a great sense of legitimacy to the mission and provides a high level of inspiration for group members. If high quality, concern for group members and community involvement is a part of a group's mission, then emphasizing the importance of quality, expressing your concern for the well being of group members, and becoming involved in community service activities are all important ways of letting others know that the organization's purpose statement is more than just a saying; it is a concept you believe in and emulate throughout your life. Leading by example is one of the strongest things you can do to ensure that the statement of purpose is not just a bunch of words printed for effect and with little substance.

♦ *Monitor Activities Surrounding the Purpose Statement.* Like most anything in life, the needs of families, businesses, and other organizations change over time. Families may need to consider change to meet the demand of a busier and faster paced culture or to consider the best way to succeed within such a culture. Businesses often change to meet the requirements of the area(s) of commerce with which they are involved. Other types of organizations often change according to the needs of those involved in or affected by the organization. In this sense, leaders need to keep careful watch to be sure that the goals and values group members set as their purpose continue to be valid and effective. You need to monitor the communication process to be certain that the group's purpose is shared often, and shared clearly, thoroughly and effectively. You need to be sure that individuals who are intimately involved with the purpose of the organization are encouraged and reinforced for their efforts, and that all efforts to this end are celebrated appropriately. Living your own life within the context of the purpose statement is critical in inspiring others and providing a living guide for others. "Walk the talk," as they say, to demonstrate to everyone that the statement of purpose of your organization is a lot more than just a neat phrase to be hung on a wall then forgotten.

A clear, strong, and effective statement of purpose is crucial to maintaining a high level of energy toward what a group hopes to accomplish and includes the values that are associated with activities designed toward meeting goals.

When was the last time you participated in a discussion of purpose regarding your work or family? What was the outcome of that discussion?

_____
_____
_____
_____
_____
_____
_____

After reviewing the list of 5 steps to improving purpose (mentioned earlier), how can you improve your purpose at work and at home?

_____
_____
_____
_____
_____
_____
_____

What are some ways to promote your purpose to others?

___
___
___
___
___
___
___

Passion Keeps the Spark of Success Glowing

Keeping focused on the group's purpose is also important, and there are lots of other activities and processes necessary for success with any group. Striving toward the organization's goals and other aspects can become mesmerizing, tiring, and frustrating. Success in any organization can become stagnant and even decline over time because leadership becomes stale and tired. We will discuss how to maintain a balanced life in a later section of the book; first, we'll outline ways to develop and keep passion toward the overall purpose of the organization as well as in other areas.

When individuals have a strong belief in the purpose a group, they often develop an intense feeling of support and commitment, and a desire to do everything possible to help realize the goals and aspirations of the group. *Passion* is created; it is not some magical feeling that just happens. Individuals must have a conviction for the purpose of a group and work consistently and diligently toward that end in spite of the hurdles experienced along the way. Group members must share a passion for their purpose in order for groups to succeed, and it is up to group leaders in families, businesses, and other organizations to help members develop and maintain the passion that is necessary for a group to be great.

> *We may affirm absolutely that nothing great in the world has been accomplished without passion.*
>
> —Hegel

The consistency and intensity of passion is often contagious, especially when that passion is communicated often and appropriately. Sometimes communication is through quiet determination and other times through zealous enthusiasm. No matter which method, a real sense of conviction is conveyed. Passion can and should be expressed through commitment to the group, its values, goals, and purpose and to individuals through genuine concern, support, and loyalty. Passion can also be expressed through the confidence that a group leader has in the purpose of the group and in the character and abilities of individual group members.

Developing and sustaining passion for the purpose of a group is critical so that group members will feel excited and fulfilled as they go about day to day tasks, activities, and responsibilities. The following is a list of suggested steps that group leaders can take in the overall development of passion in group members for the purpose of the group.

Steps to Develop Passion

- *Lead by Example/Share Your Passion with Others.* It's important to share your enthusiasm for the purpose of the group with all of those individuals in the group or connected in other ways. One way to do this is by emphasizing, through words and actions, the significance of the overall goals that the group is working. Passionate leaders often work alongside group members, championing their efforts and letting others know how important their work is. Even through difficult times, passionate leaders remain focused on the purpose of the group and their words and actions support that commitment. When others sense that passion, it helps substantiate the group's purpose and helps others grow in their own commitment. Passion is contagious and transformational, and sharing passion is one of the greatest feelings group members can experience.

> A man without passion is a fire without a light.
>
> —Chuck Gallozzi

- *Live and Lead in the Present.* Another important way to develop passion in oneself and in others is to realize the importance of living and leading in the present. We owe it to ourselves, our family, and to the organizations we are a part of to make the most of the moment. The past is important and we can use those experiences to provide us with confidence and direction, but some past experiences can be harsh and can become hurdles for success in the present and in the future, and so they need to be put into perspective.

> ### Sarah's Story
>
> There is a story about a mother and her young daughter that helps put things in perspective. The mother had been betrayed by the child's dad who, after fathering the child, denied his involvement in parenthood and actually left the area, never to be heard from again. The mother worked hard and sacrificed often for her daughter's sake and eventually became a model citizen, working in a bank, first as a teller then later as a vice president, all the while, letting the little girl know how much she was loved and how special she was. The mother taught the little girl how to care for others by volunteering with her at the local Red Cross Chapter and in their church. The mother led with passion and didn't let the past enslave her and her daughter. She lived in the present, using the past as a marker, and the future as something to look forward to.

To put it another way, the past is the past, but how we choose to use it, learn from it, or let it use us is completely up to us. It's also important to use the present to plan and prepare for the future and to remember that much of what happens tomorrow has a great deal to do with what we think, feel, and do today. Realizing the importance of *now* provides a renewed sense of energy and purpose that must be shared with those around us.

> The future is not something we enter.
> The future is something we create.
> —Leonard J. Sweet

▶ *Create an Open and Welcoming Environment.* Most of us can express our passion for things more when we feel that passion is encouraged and welcomed. Encouraging group members to share ideas, suggestions, and concerns helps others develop confidence in offering their thoughts on different areas. And when those ideas can be acted upon, it increases considerably the possibility of other ideas being offered. Lots of organizations and businesses have increased their market share significantly by conducting surveys and focus groups to ask constituents and customers what they think about the services or products being offered. This often has a dramatically positive impact on the organization if the results are used to enhance the quality of what is being offered. This same concept can and should be used with staff members, volunteers, and members of organizations, and should certainly be considered for family members. It's also important to create activities that are fun to do in safe, cheerful, and comfortable surroundings when possible; this adds interest and excitement to tasks and helps create the feeling of being *a part of something wonderful* (Boverie & Kroth, 2005)

▶ *Invite Input for Individual and Team Responsibilities.* Designing responsibilities in such a way that they seem important and even fun for individuals can be done so much more easily when the individuals involved have input as to what some of the responsibilities will be. When individuals like and value their responsibilities, they spend more time enjoying what they are doing and are more committed to quality and to their job. Finding out what others really like to do in conjunction with what needs to be done takes time on the part of the leader but it is time very well spent. In their book, *Transforming Work: The Five Keys to Achieving Trust, Commitment, and Passion in the Workplace,* authors Boverie and Kroth (2001) include working in an overly controlled setting in which you have very little to say about what you do as one of four major pitfalls that detracts from a passionate group environment. People feel complimented when asked to share input on individual and team responsibilities, groups benefit from a broader range of information, and stronger bonds develop between the leader and group members.

> **One person with passion is better than forty people merely interested.**
>
> —E.M. Forster

- *Design Tasks that Are Challenging and Meaningful.* Working on tasks that are significant to the overall purpose of a group, and understanding the importance of specific tasks are key for an individual to feel that what he/she is doing has meaning. Recognizing that what we do is making a difference in the lives of others and developing confidence in overcoming the challenges in completing tasks helps our passion grow. Leaders are charged with designing tasks that provide a sense of meaning and group members must understand and embrace that meaning. When individuals work in activities that they find boring and mundane, any potential passion is dissipated and those individuals often opt out of the group if possible. Non-meaningful work can be the number one reason individuals do not connect with a particular group. If individuals work on tasks and other activities they feel good about, and if they understand how important their success is in their lives and in the lives of others, they are more likely to be excited and motivated and feel proud of their accomplishments (Boverie and Kroth, 2001). When we are doing what we love to do, time seems to fly by; completing tasks successfully in areas we feel connected with builds confidence and even stronger commitment. Our identities merge with our accomplishments and a true sense of self efficacy and pride develops.

- *Supervise with Empowerment.* Leaders are also charged with being as certain as possible that the right individual or individuals are matched with the right tasks and with monitoring work or activities in order to adjust situations whenever necessary. Leaders also need to make sure that members are supported in being able to complete tasks realistically and successfully. Good training, demonstrations, modeling, providing examples, encouragement, and monitoring progress are all important ways to ensure that others are successful with tasks. Once individuals gain experience with various tasks, providing them with opportunities to lead and have influence themselves with certain projects is *empowering*. Empowered individuals are encouraged to use their own initiative more and can work more competently and confidently (Weis and Gantt, 2004). Individuals and teams who are encouraged to work on tasks with a certain degree of autonomy and freedom will often develop deep passion for their activities (Bennis and Townsend, 1995). Empowerment is a significant aspect of leadership and will be discussed again in another section.

♦ *Encourage, Recognize, and Celebrate Others for Their Efforts.* Acknowledging and appreciating others for their efforts in support of the group cannot be overstated, and is key in the development of passionate individuals. Relationships in any group activity are important and one of the most important relationships is between group members and leaders. Leaders must be people of influence who can be trusted for their skills and their character. Being recognized by such a leader for doing well and being encouraged to do one's best is one of the most motivational processes that can occur on the way to feeling passionate about the group's purpose. Recognition can come in many forms and the best form is the one group members prefer; a kind and grateful word, a pat on the back, a note or other preferred way of recognizing those who work effectively toward the goals of the group. Groups can also host parties and dinners to celebrate the accomplishments of their members. Passionate individuals identify with their group and their group's purpose and need to be encouraged to do the very best they can do on their way toward success. Leaders who guide and support individuals and work beside them through good times and difficult times create a transformational culture, allowing individuals to achieve higher and higher levels of success and a strong sense of belonging and accomplishments.

> *People will forget what you said, people will forget what you did, but people will never forget how you made them feel.*
>
> —Maya Angelou

Passionate individuals have a strong belief in a group's purpose; they are committed to achieving success in spite of obstacles along the way. Group members who share passion for the group's purpose are more likely to work smoothly and effectively in accomplishing goals toward success. Group leaders must be willing and able to share their passion and empower others to be consistently and highly passionate in their efforts toward the group's mission.

How passionate do you think you are for your group's purpose?

_____
_____
_____
_____
_____
_____
_____
_____

How would you describe the passion level of others in your group?

_____
_____
_____
_____
_____
_____
_____
_____

What are some of the things you can do to elevate levels of passion for your group's purpose?

_____
_____
_____
_____
_____
_____
_____
_____

How can you raise the passion level in your family?

_____
_____
_____
_____
_____
_____
_____
_____

Developing Interrelated Competencies

Character, purpose, and passion are critical for successful leadership, but it is just as important to have skills in key competency areas. Next we will look at the interrelated competency areas that strong leadership enhances.

According to the model, leaders must possess or develop an effective level of conceptual, technical, and human relationship skills to be successful, or they must be able to collaborate with those who are competent in these three areas. But what exactly do these competency areas mean? How can these competencies be developed? And how can they be integrated into leadership at home and at work?

Understanding and Developing Conceptual Competencies

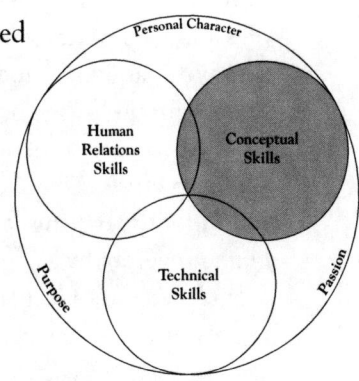

Conceptual skills or *competencies* are usually associated with the critical thinking side of a person and include vision, decision making, and problem solving. A conceptual competency is, in effect, a theoretical competency; in spite of that, there are substantive processes designed to develop conceptual attributes.

Vision Serves as Focus and Inspiration

> Where there is no vision, the people perish.
> —Prov.29:18 (KJV)

This bold and clear statement strongly implies that organizations and families need a direction to focus their resources and attention. In 1989, Steven Covey wrote the *7 Habits of Highly Effective People* and Habit No. 2 was "Begin with the end in mind." In effect, Covey was saying that individuals need to envision the end of their life and project how they would like to be remembered; as a family member, an organizational member, and as a community member.

Covey suggests there are two steps in visioning. The first step involves a mental picture; the second is more physical. The mental picture includes a vision of what a family or organization is about, where each unit needs to be headed, and a plan that could make the vision a reality. It is similar to a contractor working with a blueprint. Before the foundation can be set and the walls can be put up, there needs to be a blueprint that includes these two aspects along with many, many others.

He wrote that you need to begin every day, every relationship, and every activity envisioning what you hope that scenario will become, then plan and try to act accordingly. And like building a house with a blueprint, the structure may change from the original design but only if the parties agree to change it or if there is an error in implementation. Covey went on to state that individuals should develop a *principle centered vision*, in which the vision is based in part on the principles and values that guide our lives. This vision should be a shared vision in which we invite our family members, organizational members, and community members to offer input.

According to Senge (1990), "A vision is truly shared when you and I have a similar picture and are committed to one another having it, not just to each of us, individually, having it. When people truly share a vision, they are connected, bound together by a common inspiration" (p. 206). So not only does a shared vision provide a focus, but it is also motivational because we become excited about working toward the same goals. Incorporating aspects of the *invitational leadership* model and the *servant leadership* model could also be helpful in developing a shared vision. Both models encourage active involvement of individuals in the leadership process.

One of the most respected authors of our time on the subject of leadership is John Maxwell who made *vision* a key quality of a leader in his book *The Indispensable Qualities of a Leader* (1999). According to Maxwell, vision starts within us and we need to be able to recognize our calling and sometimes partner with someone with a similar vision (a shared vision) and the aptitude to help us make things happen. Maxwell went on to say that vision is not a mystical quality but rather is born from our experiences in the past. He states that vision is far reaching and to be truly effective it must add value to the lives of others. Maxwell concluded with the idea that if the vision is clear and appealing, and is communicated thusly, it will attract and unite people. Individuals must feel good about taking part in the vision of a family or organization. That helps develop a collaborative commitment toward mutual goals and in the development of a group's *purpose*, which we discussed in an earlier section.

Developing a shared vision with others can be as simple as collecting and assessing ideas and information. Round-table discussions at home, business lunches at work, interviews and surveys with constituents; all contribute to the knowledge base of what the vision of a group could or should be. Usually the ideas are already pretty much there; they just have to be requested and assimilated, then followed by open and flexible discussions regarding the direction in which the group wishes to go. And that direction or vision may sometimes need to be re-tooled, depending on changing needs and circumstances.

A good example of this process occurred when the Scandinavian Airline System (SAS) began to rework their vision or mission statement back in the mid 1990s and they started by surveying their business class customers. Business travelers fly quite a bit more than most others and they usually can afford higher fares. SAS assimilated the information they gathered and implemented programs and amenities based on the surveys, resulting in unparalleled success (Kotter, 1995).

> *If one advances confidently in the direction of his dreams, and endeavors to live the life which he has imagined, he will meet with a success unexpected in common hours.*
>
> —Henry David Thoreau

One important thing to keep in mind is to value the ideas of others and treat each idea as if it might become a part of the overall vision of the group. Stephen Covey's Habit No. 5 was "*Seek first to understand then to be understood*" (1989) in which he describes the importance of genuinely listening and trying to understand the thoughts and feelings of others prior to developing an overall vision. If others perceive you as having a real interest in their opinions, a trusting relationship ensues and ideas can really start flowing.

When individuals share a vision and a desire, have effective tools, knowledge, and enthusiasm, there is almost nothing they can't accomplish.

Reflection & Application

Make it a point to sit down with family and work team members and discuss the vision of your family or the work group. Is it a shared vision and how so?

_____
_____
_____
_____
_____
_____
_____
_____
_____

How does your current vision at home or work guide what you do as a group?

_____
_____
_____
_____
_____
_____
_____
_____

Does it need revision? If so, what is your plan for revision?

Effective Decision Making Leads Us toward Success

Making the right decisions in various matters is just as important as having enlightened and strong vision. *Decision making* is important, time consuming, and complicated for families and for organizations and making appropriate decisions can make all the difference in the world in moving toward success.

Because decision making is so important, there are five tenets we would like you to consider prior to getting involved with a decision-making process.

Five Tenets as a Prequel to Decision Making

1. Just like vision, make important decisions *principle centered*. Principle-centered decisions are made with the values of the family or organization in mind as ideas and alternatives are considered. Values like *respect, responsibility, fairness,* and *integrity* should always be considered when making important decisions.

    Respecting individuals who may be involved in a decision-making process and those who may be affected by the process is critical in leading with character. Realizing and accepting responsibility for each decision made provides added incentive to make the best decisions possible. Maintaining fairness for all of those involved in decisions can be challenging but it needs to be a goal we strive for. And finally, we along with others, need to be able to be trusted that we are making the best decisions possible and that our level of integrity is high.

> It's not hard to make decisions when you know what your values are.
>
> —Roy Disney

2. Concentrate on the big picture or the *purpose* of the family or organization when making a decision. For instance, sometimes one decision may seem in conflict with another, so it is important for everyone that the vision of the family or organization is reviewed as often as possible and reasonable. Decision, therefore, will more likely be made according to the overall goals of the group.

   As we mentioned earlier, the vision or purpose of a group can change depending on variables such as changing needs and circumstances, so it is also important to revisit the vision to ensure that everyone is on the same page and that decisions are based on what is believed to be the overall purpose of the group.

3. *Invite* as many individuals to be a part of the decision-making process as is possible and realistic. Inviting others to be a part of important decision making provides more input and energy, and gives each person a sense that they are a valued member of the team. Involving others is often a *transformational* process, because individuals are interacting and developing a synergy to make healthy, enlightened decisions. It is certainly an *invitational* process in that respect and caring are an aspect of being invited to the table. And it can even be considered a *servant leadership* concept, because the leader is asking others what they are wishing for in the decision-making process.

   Decisions that involve more of those individuals that should be involved have a much better chance of developing into results that are *win/win*. This is because few individuals are left out of having input in the overall process and, therefore, there is less chance that someone's position will be neglected. Including those individuals necessary to the decision making process takes intelligence, insight, and sometimes even courage, but the results can go a long way in establishing a foundation of trust, involvement, and success.

4. *Emotion* is invariably a part of the decision-making process and should not be taken lightly. Understanding the emotions that individuals possess during the making of a decision is very important. If someone has a high level of passion for a particular direction he/she wishes the group to move toward, then that passion should be considered. Is it a passion born out of significant insight and knowledge? Or is it a passion representative of strong, personal desire?

If the feeling is perceived to be one of insight and knowledge, then that passion should be considered as a significant part of the decision-making process. But if it appears to be one based mostly on personal needs or direction then it probably shouldn't be considered as strongly.

5. *Leadership* style plays a significant part in determining how decisions are to be made and how successful the results will be. Should a leader make a decision independently of a group? Or should group members be involved in the decision? Studies and literature suggest that allowing entire groups make decisions takes more time and energy, but the decisions are more readily accepted and the results of the decisions will be implemented more effectively (Vroom, 1995).

Some decisions require a quicker turn around or may best be left in the hands of a few individuals; such decisions can also be effective if evaluated and implemented carefully. But a leader who is more often than not inviting and democratic will be more likely to have a decision-making process that is well received and implemented, and more likely to have group members that feel like they are a real part of the overall team.

The tenets outlined above provide a good foundation of thought prior to the actual decision-making process because they encourage us to reflect on important considerations that add quality to the overall process. Most experts in the area of leadership and decision making promote a step-by-step process. Depending on the expert, the steps could range anywhere from 3 to 20 or more in number. One concept promoted by management editor, consultant, and university president and chancellor E. Frank Harrison includes a six step process that's simple yet profound in its potential (1983). Remember to review the tenets prior to using the decision-making process developed by Harrison and to fold those tenets into the process when appropriate.

6-Step Decision-Making Process

Step 1: *Setting Objectives.* A family or organizational group must first agree on their objectives (*purpose*). The more involved individuals are in the setting of objectives, the more likely they will be to believe in those objectives and to work hard toward achieving them.

Step 2: *Searching for Alternatives.* This part of the decision-making process calls for thorough research for information relating to the objectives under consideration. Researching information internally within the group should be a priority, but researching information from outside the group can also prove to be valuable. Once all of the information is assimilated, then group members can suggest possible alternatives in making a decision.

Step 3: *Comparing and Evaluating Alternatives.* All reasonable alternatives should be considered. Each alternative decision must be evaluated alone or in combination based on anticipated outcomes. Anticipated outcomes should not only focus on the objectives of the group but also on the group's values.

Step 4: *The Act of Choice.* One of the most challenging parts in making a decision is determining which alternative will have the best outcome. Experience, history, knowledge, and team work should also play into the formula of making a decision from a number of alternatives.

Step 5: *Implementing the Decision.* Once a decision has been reached, it is necessary to take steps to put the decision into action. This shifts the process from a conceptual process to an operational process. Each person involved in the decision making should be made aware that the decision is being implemented.

Step 6: *Follow-up and Monitoring.* The implementation of a decision needs to be monitored throughout to ensure that it is meeting the objective(s). Some decisions will need to be fine tuned or changed altogether during the operational process, and it is important for a leader to recognize when this may be necessary and to discuss these changes with others.

Making the right kinds of decisions is crucial to having successful groups.

Have your decisions in the past been *principle centered* decisions? Explain:

___

How can you incorporate more *principle centered* decisions into your future decision-making process?

___

Would you like to invite more individuals to the decision-making process? Who should they be?

_____
_____
_____
_____
_____
_____

Which of the concepts on decision making can be most helpful to you, now or in the future?

_____
_____
_____
_____
_____
_____
_____

Solving Problems with Others

Problems in any family or organization are inevitable, and there are as many ways to solve problems as there are ways to make good, strong decisions. We would like to guide you toward some of the more proven problem-solving techniques, as well as ways to solve problems as a team. Because problems are inevitable, the more effective a group is in solving problems the stronger their bond should become and, as a result, the more successful the family or organization will become.

The act of working through problems often becomes developmental cornerstones for individuals and for groups. Although sometimes appealing, a life of "least resistance" can often lead to a life without challenge and without opportunities to develop character, strength, stamina, and determination. It could lead to groups of individuals without real testing of mettle and therefore without bonding, camaraderie, and success.

Often, the things that challenge us in life become the things that help make us who we are. Helen Keller was challenged by unbelievable disabilities but worked through them with the help of Anne Sullivan to become a leader and mentor to thousands of others with disabilities. Martin Luther King, Jr. was challenged by a system of racism and injustice but worked through it, and, with the help of like-minded individuals, he became the pinnacle example of an individual striving for justice and fairness for all. Lance Armstrong was stricken with cancer, an emotionally and physically crippling illness. In spite of this perilous dilemma, Armstrong worked through his health issues, went on to become the king of cycling for his successes in the Tour de France, and galvanized an entire society in generating over $50 million in funds toward cancer research.

All three of these individuals had the same thing in common; they each faced unbelievably challenging situations. Instead of giving up and running away or hiding from them, they faced the issues head on developed plans to meet the challenges, and worked with others with a similar intent. The results of facing challenges with a strong plan and a great team as support can be unbelievable.

Developing a good structure and a great team is the idea behind our three step plan for avoiding or managing problems:

1. *Be Proactive.* Recognizing situations with potential to become problematic and addressing the situation before problems actually occur is valuable.

By remaining cognizant of potential eventualities, good leaders develop a sense of possible and sometimes probable consequences. One way this sense is heightened is by involving others in assessing various scenarios and determining potential hazards. Effective leaders keep an open mind; they encourage others to participate in the review of potential downfalls even if certain opinions run counter to popular ways of thinking. They hold meetings to discuss concerns and try to head bad things off at the pass.

Establishing preventive safeguards for procedures and activities can be a very effective way to anticipate problems and head them off. Trying to involve as many people as possible in establishing safeguards is an important step. The more family and organizational members are involved in establishing ways to prevent problems, the stronger they will feel about the safeguards and the more likely they will be to follow them.

2. **Think Outside the Box.** Many problems can be addressed with "tried and proven processes" that have worked in the past. But not every problem can be solved in predictable ways. Sometimes it takes stretching the imagination and taking chances, and trying things that seem different or unusual but may have the potential to resolve certain situations. Almost every family, business, or organization will have to try something different and new to work out some future problems. Leonardo da Vinci was far from an ordinary thinker, to say the least. He established several principles to consider when working on problems (Gelb, 1998):

- Maintain a strong and curious approach to life and never allow yourself to stop learning.
- Remain open to testing your thoughts through experience and be willing to learn from mistakes.
- Keep your senses alive in order to fully experience, appreciate, and learn from life.
- Don't shy away from uncertainty and paradox; some of life's greatest discoveries occur through assessing all possibilities.
- Try to have a balance between artistic, creative endeavors and more logical, scientific endeavors in order to become a well- rounded individual.
- In the face of adversity, try to maintain a sense of grace, poise, and fitness.
- Recognize and appreciate the interconnectedness of all things.

da Vinci was convinced that incorporating one or more of these principles in problem solving situations could be very effective. Thinking outside the box as da Vinci suggests often leads to unusual responses to difficult problems, which may result in the best way to address certain situations.

3. **Use a Problem-Solving Process.** In addition to being proactive and stepping outside the box to manage problems, it's a very good idea to incorporate a proven process in problem-solving situations. The following process was developed in large part by Maxwell (1993) and provides guidelines for handling problem situations:

- *Identify and Understand the Problem.* Some situations seem to plague us because we have not fully recognized or understood the significance of a problem. "The devil really is in the details" is often proved true; we need to understand the parameters of a problem well before we can begin to address something adequately. Because each individual brings different insights, knowledge, and opinions to the table, it is imperative that individuals involved with a problem be invited to help identify the problem; to define its overall significance as well as its details.

  The process of sitting down with family members or organizational or business colleagues, expressing the idea that a problem may exist, and then developing a group mindset as to what the problem may be and its finer points is a major factor in working toward a solution or a way to manage the situation.

- *Prioritize the Problem.* Most families and organizations are juggling lots and lots of balls at once and problems have a way of appearing at inopportune times. So once a problem has been identified and understood by a group, it will need to be prioritized. Some problems are important to address immediately; other problems may need more time for study or may not be as pressing. If a problem is relegated to a back burner but it has been identified by a group as important, then it is imperative that a time period for addressing the problem be understood and that group members are kept abreast of the ongoing status of the problem.

- *Select Effective Team Members.* It's true; some problems can easily be managed alone. But if the problem is significant, it is important to invite the right individuals to be a part of the team for a number of reasons. Individuals who are involved in the problem-solving process will feel as if they are valued. They will bring a variety of ideas to the table about the causes of the problem(s) and ways to manage the problem. Once a solution is formed, they will be more enthusiastic about implementing the solution.

Individuals who are involved in the problem should be included in problem solving, as well as those group members with necessary expertise. Personal character also needs to be considered. Are they individuals who can combine reason and logic with a passion to work on problematic situations? And, as da Vinci would say, consider thinking "outside the box" when it comes to individuals who may help in certain situations.

- *Determine Causes and Problem-Solving Solutions.* With a team in place, you can begin to "brain-storm" ideas about the overriding causes of the problem(s) under consideration. In a brain-storming session, it is a good idea to let all opinions be heard and registered before going over the list. Thorough research is encouraged so that no stone is left unturned. Individuals outside the immediate group should also be considered; if the problem is significant and requires a special expertise, consultants and problem-solving specialists should always be considered for family or organizational problems.

- *Explore Solutions.* Once the core of a problem is understood, it's time to encourage team members to explore as many ways as possible to manage the problem and then to express those ideas. Again, brain storming is a great process for putting lots of ideas on the table without being critiqued or shot down too soon. Leaders need to encourage team members to feel comfortable in making suggestions.

- *Prioritize, Select, and Implement the Most Effective Solution.* Careful and thorough research plus including the best team members to participate in the problem-solving process should lead to a list of strong, potential solutions. Maxwell (1993) suggests that the leader then ask the following questions:

Which solution has the greatest potential for effectiveness?

Which solution will be most helpful for the family/organization?

Which solution has momentum and feasibility?

Which solution has the greatest chance to work?

Once there is general agreement among group members as to the most effective way to handle a problem, the next step is to develop a plan to implement the solution as soon as it is reasonable. It's imperative that individuals assigned action steps to manage or solve a problem implement those steps quickly, and keep other members informed.

◆ *Evaluate and Monitor the Solution.* Deciding on a solution to a problem doesn't necessarily mean that it will be effective or work as planned. Also, variables associated with a problem can change at any moment. So it is critical that the leader and team members keep a watchful eye on the progress of the solution and that adjustments are initiated if and when necessary. It is also important that a solution process be afforded enough time to determine its worthiness. It's sometimes a delicate balance and setting group meetings at specific junctures to measure progress is a great idea.

Solving problems with others provides opportunities for more ideas to be considered and often provides a chance for bonding among team members. The process can help strengthen confidence in one another and the group as a working body. Problems are inevitable, but like an old friend once said, "It's not the number of flat tires you have in life that matters, what's important is how well you fix 'em!"

> The way I see it, if you want the rainbow you gotta put up with the rain.
> —Dolly Parton

What are some recent problems your group or family has had to address?

___

What methods were used to manage these problems?

___

Which methods were successfully employed, and can they be used in the future?

_____
_____
_____
_____
_____
_____
_____

How can the problem-solving processes discussed in this section be helpful in the future?

_____
_____
_____
_____
_____
_____
_____
_____
_____
_____

Understanding and Developing Technical Competencies

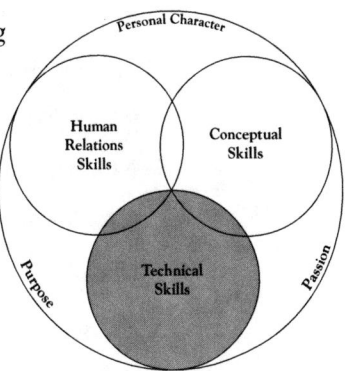

Conceptual thinking is important in developing vision, decision making, and problem solving, but technical skills or competencies are the nuts, bolts, and tools that are crucial in putting the visions, decisions, and solutions together. Several technical competencies that are interconnected with both home and work include planning, empowerment, budgeting and stewardship, and personal balance.

Planning with Skill and Purpose

There is an old saying that goes, "The best made plans of mice and men often go astray." Although this is sometimes true, effective planning can make all the difference in the world in the successes associated with any family or organization.

The quality of activities, projects, services, and products often indicates how effective family and organizational members are in the planning process. Effective planning involves asking family members, organizational members, and constituents what they hope for with certain activities, services, and products. A *People Centered/Benefits Approach* to planning implies that leaders strive to develop activities, projects, or products that not only meet the expectations of the individuals involved but can even exceed them and provide a positive outcome (Weis and Gantt, 2004). Quality activities, projects, and products must be carefully planned, implemented, and evaluated. Effective planning should include a step-by-step process, although the sequence and number of steps may vary from activity to activity and project to project:

1. **Select a Planning Team.** Including a number of different individuals on the planning team often results in greater creativity, synergy, and expertise. Groups have greater possibilities for comprehensive planning than do individuals and these groups should include:

- Family and/or organizational members with specific expertise of the activity, project, or product
- Family members, organizational members, or constituents who are involved with or who stand to benefit from the activity, project, or product
- Consultants or others with specific expertise in the area of interest

Planning committee members should be responsible for the following:

- Develop a schedule for meetings
- Identify and prioritize a sequence of planning steps
- Assign individuals to coordinate each step
- Implement, monitor, and adjust plans when necessary
- Discuss and evaluate results

2. ***Find Out What People Need and Want.*** Before planning activities, projects, or products, it is smart to ensure that what individuals need or want is clear and understood. *Needs* are usually understood to be deficiencies in areas of physiological, psychological, or social imbalance. When an individual recognizes a deficiency in any of these areas, it is considered a need (Edginton and Ford 1985). Physiological needs can include food, water, sleep, or sex; psychological or social needs can include companionship, recognition, social interaction, self-esteem, love, and achievements (Weis and Gantt, 2004). *Desires*, which are defined as wishes perceived as needs, should also be considered in planning projects and products.

There is a grocery store in the northeastern part of the United States whose owners sit down with customers on an ongoing basis in a focus-group setting. They ask the customers what they think of current items and services, and what they might like in the way of new items or services. They implement as many of the suggestions from their customers as is reasonable. This attention to what their constituents want has resulted in a significantly increased business over the past several decades.

A needs assessment can help determine what family members believe is important regarding their daily lives and beyond. It can help determine if organizational members are feeling fulfilled in their roles and what organizational constituents or customers value in the context of services and products.

There are at least two effective processes for determining needs and desires and both should be considered: (1) Leaders need to assess existing data that include published reports in magazines, newspapers, journals, and other informational venues. (2) Assessing the needs and desires of family and organizational members and constituents firsthand can be done through informal and/or formal interviews, focus groups, and even surveys. Interviews and focus groups can provide quite a lot of information, and surveys provide an opportunity for constituents to offer suggestions and ideas with some anonymity.

Many businesses have individuals and departments that conduct needs assessments or they work with consultants to find out what their constituents and/or employees are thinking. Family leaders can hold meetings from time to time to see what members are thinking about. More information on conducting a needs assessment can be found by researching community resources through the Better Business Bureau, the United Way, or local colleges or universities. You can also find information on conducting a needs assessment in the book, *Knowledge and Skill Development in Nonprofit Organizations* by Weis and Gantt (2004).

3. *Incorporate Values and Mission in the Planning Process.* Any time a family or an organization of any kind is in the planning process, it is very important to consider the principles (values) that guide the family or organization and the mission. Holding true to such values as *respect*, *fairness*, and *integrity* when planning an activity, service, or product means that the group remains focused on core values while deciding what's important regarding initiatives for the future. Too many families and organizations get blindsided by exciting opportunities or by unforeseen hurdles, and begin to violate the values that they have thus far held close.

A similar kind of thing happens when groups decide to go in a different direction because of similar scenarios and end up totally off track from the overall purpose of the group. This kind of mindset can divide groups into factions and create turmoil and conflict. Diversification from an original mission can turn out to be a positive thing, however, if the team members are brought into the process to discuss and decided on diversification.

4. *Determine the Objectives of Planning at the Start.* Each activity, service, or product should have clear, understandable outcomes or objectives agreed upon by group members at the start and clearly communicated throughout. Having understandable and realistic objectives provides a

focus, a motivation, and a means to look back and measure the success of the planning group. Depending on the group and the purpose, this can be fairly informal or highly structured. Because situations sometimes change and some variables are unforeseen, it may also be important to allow for some flexibility in meeting objectives.

5. **Identify the Kinds of Resources Needed.** Conducting or developing any activity, service, or product will require resources to some extent, so it's important to determine what is already available and what is needed. Each initiative will vary, of course, but resource categories often include the following (Weis and Gantt, 2004):

- *Space Availability.* Evaluate the kind of space that may be needed for the initiative. Existing space is often the best and least expensive alternative but other space(s) may be necessary depending on the circumstances

- *Personnel.* In some cases family members and organizational members are all that are needed for future activities, projects, or products; other times, outside consultants and experts must also be considered.

- *Finances.* Some initiatives require little operating money and others require a great deal. Conduct exhaustive research to determine how to get the most success from the least amount of money, and the best source of financial support.

- *Supplies.* Determining the kinds and quantities of necessary supplies is integral to being successful in every planning process.

- *Equipment.* Another important consideration for success is the kind and number of specific equipment necessary to make the plans a reality.

6. **Make Risk Management Priority No. 1.** Every activity, service, or product will inevitably involve risk; businesses have product recalls because of production errors and families encounter hazards every day at home, in the community, or on the highway. The purpose of risk management is to do everything possible to keep risk at the lowest possible level. A *risk* is considered anything that may impede the purpose of a group and may include potential and real threats to individuals, income, property, or reputation (Weis and Gantt, 2004).

A classic list of strategies for handling risks was developed by Van der Smissen in 1990 and still holds strong value today. Van der Smissen's suggests three components to managing risks:

- *Identification of Risk.* Before anything can be done to eliminate risks, they must be identified. There are obvious and less obvious risks, so a careful and thorough assessment during the identification component of risk management is important. For instance, family members vacationing in a mountainous area should already know to hike together and have the proper equipment, supplies, and plans for different circumstances. However, certain types of terrain and sudden, unforeseen weather conditions can result in some perilous situations.

- *Evaluation of Risk.* Once risks have been effectively identified, they need to be evaluated for potential occurrence, severity, and level of consequence should an accident, injury, or illness actually happen.

- *Handling Risk.* Van der Smissen proposes three basic ways to handle risk:
  (1) *Prevention (Avoidance).* Ensuring that individuals have adequate training and knowledge regarding an activity, service, or product is an important way to prevent bad experiences.
  (2) *Risk Reduction.* Clearly communicating safety rules and policies with individuals and maintaining good procedures of risk reduction will go a long way to keep risk to a minimum. Rules and policies need to be continually monitored by leaders.
  (3) *Risk Retention or Transfer.* Once a family or an organization has decided to continue with an activity, service, or product, it is important to have a plan or a means to transfer some of the loss to another institution, such as an insurance company, should a loss occur.

Experts at a nonprofit risk management center propose four somewhat different strategies for managing risks (1997):

- *Avoidance.* Families and organizations may choose not to develop some activities, services, or products because they are deemed from the outset to be too risky or may seem too awesome or overpowering in total. Here is when another strategy, modification, can be considered.

- *Modification.* This indicates that an activity, service, or product is accepted as important and all agree it should be implemented but limits are placed on various aspects. . For instance, a swimming pool would be great fun for a family but all agree that installation should be delayed until all of the family members reach a certain age, are fully able to swim, and strong adult supervision is available. A nonprofit organization that transports members from place to place may consider putting limits on the transportation system such as verifying the licensing and safety records of all drivers, requiring safe-driver training program, implementing a program for regular vehicular inspections and maintenance (Weis and Gantt, 2004).

- *Retention.* Certain procedures or products may be deemed worth the inherent risks involved. In this case, families and organizations must be prepared to handle those risks should they become a reality. They need to assess the potential for each risk and determine the consequences and associated loss should it actually occur. This risk assessment should be on-going as situations change over time and the level of risks can change along with potential outcomes.

- *Sharing.* Transferring some of the risks involved with an activity or product to another organization or institution such as an insurance company is an important and common way to "share" the burden of various risks. Families and organizations should look carefully at the strengths and limitations of such institutions prior to making a commitment. Caution is needed, as transferring the complete burden or responsibility of a situation to another entity is impossible. For instance, a business may believe they have appropriate liability insurance for accidents, but the policy will not cover the damage to the organization's reputation should a "preventable" accident occur.

Risks are unavoidable and can never be completely managed away, but families, organizations, and businesses need to make risk management one of the highest priorities in any and all endeavors. Keeping risk to a minimum and developing ways to effectively manage risk can make a huge difference in whether or not a family or an organization is successful.

> A ship in the harbor is usually safe;
> but that's not what ships are built for.
>
> —African Proverb

7. ***Communicate and Promote Projects.*** As ideas and plans begin to take shape, it is important to share information and to communicate within the group as well as outside the group in many cases. Families that plan vacation trips together need to share information on destinations, purposes, and logistics to reduce the possibility of unfortunate surprises as much as possible. Sharing such information through family meetings can help to develop bonding and ensure happier experiences overall. Sharing information with relatives, neighbors, and travel professionals can also be essential in some circumstances. A comprehensive checklist of people to contact, tasks to address, things to pack, and individuals responsible for different aspects of the trip can be invaluable.

    Promoting services and products for organizations and businesses is essential. Most businesses have their own marketing or public relations department or hire consultants to present their products or services in the best possible way. Organizations form committees to develop public service announcements, flyers, web sites, for example, to create a stir about an upcoming service that needs to be shared with constituents. Marketing departments at colleges and universities can often be helpful in assisting nonprofit organizations and small businesses.

8. ***Develop a Project Budget.*** Successful families and organizations often realize the importance of a budget. A *project budget* is nothing more than a projection of the *estimated expenses* that are associated with a particular project and the *estimated income or revenue* that are a part of a project. These estimated expenses might include materials, supplies, rental space, travel, personnel, food, and telephone costs , for example. Families have to determine whether additional money is needed to cover the cost for planned activities such as vacations or whether the cost can be covered by existing funds. The same is true for an organization or a business. They can sometimes pay for services and products from an existing budgeted income line or they may have to develop other ways of income production, often through the project or service itself.

    Keeping records of actual expenses and sources of income for each project provide great information that will help determine if similar initiatives are warranted in the future. Even though some projects turn out as deficit spending and have to be paid for through other revenue generating activities, they may still be considered worthwhile for the results and the experience.

9. **Conduct a Project Walk-Through/Rehearsal.** Prior to conducting any activity or service or developing any product, it is a great idea to conduct a visual and even physical walk-through or rehearsal to examine as many aspects of the project as possible. If it is a significant event or project, this sort of visualizing and assessing might need to be occur numerous times. Visualizing what might happen and assessing all that might be needed for a project can be a very valuable tool in keeping that project on the pathway toward success. A walk-through or rehearsal allows group members opportunities to study procedures and assess most considerations. It allows them time to review the overall plan prior to implementation and suggest changes if and when necessary.

10. **Implement, Monitor, and Evaluate the Project.** Once the "i"s are dotted and the "t"s are crossed, it is time to put things into full swing. Plans provide guidelines for how to proceed with a project. This step in the process is when the plans become a reality and leaders and other participants make things happen Returning to Part I of this book and reviewing some of the leadership concepts may be a good way for leaders to ensure that character and quality are incorporated into the leadership process. As soon as a project is off the ground, it's time to immediately begin monitoring the progress of the project.

    Both monitoring and evaluating can be done informally or formally. For families, observation and discussion are often all that are needed to assess the effectiveness of an activity. Family leaders must be sure they incorporate a process called *active listening and understanding* in the monitoring process. During active listening, a leader reflects back to someone what the leader perceives the speaker has said. This helps to encourage a more meaningful and realistic communication process regarding the progress of an activity.

    Businesses and organizations may monitor the progress of a project in more formal ways—through interviews, focus groups, and surveys, for instance—and they can use the same process for evaluating a service or product once it is completed. No activity, service, or product is above improvement and so monitoring and evaluating projects is critical to the success of any group.

> *Setting a goal is not the main thing.*
> *It is deciding how you will go about achieving*
> *it and staying with that plan.*
>
> —Tom Landry

11. ***Record Results and Formulate Recommendations for the Future.*** Conducting good evaluation processes provides valuable information that can be used for the future. Keeping records and documents about the successes of family activities and initiatives can provide family members with important information. Documentation on trips, renovation projects, repair work, school reports, health matters, and many other areas is essential for family members to stay informed so they can make good decisions in the future. Organizations and businesses often maintain records on their projects for the same reason—to stay informed of their successes and to see where changes might need to be made in the future.

    Making recommendations on future initiatives based on past experiences allow groups an opportunity to explore possibilities from an enlightened position. Such recommendations should be readily available to all group members to assist in future planning endeavors.

    Strong leaders understand the importance of planning for the success of any group project or initiative. As we mentioned in the beginning of this section, the steps we discussed do not necessarily need to be in the exact sequence given here, and not all of the steps need to be considered for all projects.

Reflection & Application

Think about some upcoming projects or activities you have in mind.

Which of the steps discussed earlier would you like to include in your planning process?

_____
_____
_____
_____
_____
_____
_____
_____

Which of these do you believe are most important? Why?

_____
_____
_____
_____
_____
_____
_____
_____

Are there additional steps that you believe to be necessary for successful planning? What are they?

_____
_____
_____
_____
_____
_____
_____
_____

Empower Others with Encouragement, Education, and Training

One of the most important and exciting things leaders can do is to *empower* members of their group to become more confident, competent, and self-reliant individuals. Sharing power or authority with others is a process of empowerment and, in effect, allows others to develop influence—a key concept in the leadership process.

Empowered individuals feel as if they are supported and encouraged by their leaders, and often perceive themselves as having a sense of control and being somewhat free to operate independently. Empowered individuals often feel a strong sense of pride in the accomplishments of their group, and develop a deep commitment to the group's purpose and are highly motivated toward reaching that purpose (Edginton, Hudson, and Ford 1999).

Before a leader can adequately empower others, the leader must be empowered him- or herself, and must be able to share critical aspects of family and/or organizational and corporate life. They must be able and willing to encourage and support others to develop their own talents and skills. Strong leaders have the knowledge, confidence, and desire to enable others; that is, they feel comfortable providing training and encouragement to help develop leadership potential in others. In a sense, the leader takes on the role of a coach who trusts individuals to work well within a clearly defined framework without close supervision, and who reflects with individuals on progress of various projects (Eisenberg and Goodall, Jr., 2004) Empowered individuals are encouraged to have contrary views from the mainstream and to use their sense of empowerment to transform the group with which they are involved.

Empowerment includes the sharing of power or influence and decision making, and this usually occurs through a process of delegating and motivating individuals to a level of self efficacy (Eisenberg and Goodall, Jr., 2004). Although an empowered person has a healthy sense of freedom that can result in a great deal of creativity, a clear sense of parameters and boundaries still needs to be understood by the individual and the leader. As a leader learns more about the character and abilities of an individual, then the boundaries may expand or contract under certain circumstances.

There is a danger in delegating too much too quickly and in delegating with too little supervision. Individuals in this situation may often feel overwhelmed and lack the confidence and competencies to work on a project effectively. Too little supervision or lack of a monitoring system can have dire consequences as well. There is also the danger in delegating too little too late. Some individuals are ready, willing, and able to take the reins of a certain project but a leader is unable or unwilling to allow that individual the opportunity to take the initiative. This often results in an individual who feels stifled and frustrated with the group.

The most effective delegation comes when leaders take the time to sit down with individuals to ask questions and develop a keen sense of an individual's motivation and competencies. The leader can then decide how much freedom or control an individual needs, and will be able to adjust that level when the situation calls for it (Hersey and Blanchard, 1977).

Delegation within any activity or project, which can lead to feelings of empowerment, should only occur after individuals have been effectively educated and trained in the areas of interest and involvement, and when both the leader and individual are aware of certain established or developing competencies. And because everything is changing at such a rapid pace, leaders need to maintain ongoing training so that individuals can continuously learn and develop. It is also important to remember that individuals learn in different ways and at different speeds, and a good leader will make the effort to suit the needs of the individual (Eisenberg and Goodall, Jr., 2004).

> Education is not the filling of a pail but the lighting of a fire.
> —William Butler Yates

During training, a leader must maintain good, direct communication to assess where an individual is in the learning process and the individual's motivation level regarding each task or project. This provides the leader with knowledge to help determine what level of trust and freedom an individual should have initially. Ongoing communication will help determine when that level of freedom needs to be increased or pulled back. Another important piece of the empowerment package is to offer rewards to individuals when they have been successfully trained and empowered, and the results are expressed through successful accomplishments.

Leaders in families and even businesses cannot always provide the right kind of education and training for each situation, and so many families and organizations often rely on others for teaching, coaching, and consulting. As a matter of fact, professional trainers are sometimes in a better position to determine in what areas individuals need training and are better prepared to offer that training. It is critical that leaders carefully select those who are providing educational and skill development support.

A father or mother may not be able to teach their child how to be the best gymnast possible, but they can certainly guide her to a coach with great knowledge and character. They can then support the child in her efforts and empower her as her talents grow. A school administrator may not have the capacity to provide faculty members with the knowledge and skills necessary to teach with technological competency, but he/she can contract with a proven business in the field to be certain that faculty members are competent in that integral part of teaching and learning.

Before any plan of action is determined, it is best to sit down with the parties involved and identify the areas requiring education and training. Brain storming and other discussion methods can help determine what individuals need and want in the context of training and support. The leaders should discuss the various alternatives for delivering the best education and training system(s), then choose the system that seems to work best. Like other decisions, the chosen alternative needs to be monitored and evaluated for value and possible modification or change.

As long as it is implemented well, empowering others within a group is one of the most important and exhilarating things that a leader can do. Empowered individuals are more competent and confident; they usually feel a stronger sense of freedom, independence, and creativity, and they maintain a stronger commitment to the mission of the group. Working together, empowered individuals often achieve success beyond expectations.

What are you currently doing to empower individuals in your work group or family?

_____
_____
_____
_____
_____
_____
_____
_____
_____

How successful do you think these processes are and why do you think that?

_____
_____
_____
_____
_____
_____
_____
_____
_____

What are additional ways in which you could empower others even more?

Budgeting and Stewardship of Resources

Because we all have limited resources, budgeting or a plan that projects how much income or revenue we will need to operate and how much money we plan to spend is critical. Before going through a step-by-step process for developing a budget, we present a few important tenets to keep in mind while thinking about the budgeting process. Remember that family and organizational leaders don't necessarily have to be experts in all three competency areas including budgeting as long as they are willing to collaborate with those who have that expertise.

1. Prior to developing a budget the leader needs to sit down with group members and discuss the *principles* and the *purpose* that the organization has developed so that it will be easier to establish priorities for financial matters in the future. A leader that is concerned about the environment, for instance, should consider environmental variables in making financial decisions for a family or a business to maintain a high level of integrity.

    A family that is very interested in higher education for the children must concentrate on details regarding the cost of the education and ways to cover that cost, while maintaining a life style that keeps everyone healthy and happy. A business leader with a vision for diversification and expansion must consider ways to cover the cost of the expansion while maintaining current operations.

2. As reflected in many other parts of this book, significant consideration should be given about whom to *invite* to the budgeting planning process and whose input would generally be welcomed. Family members that are

> And the Lord God took the man,
> and put him into the Garden of Eden
> to dress it and to keep it.
>
> —Genesis 2:15 (KJV)

asked their opinions on financial matters will feel more self-efficacy especially if their input is genuinely considered. Additionally, each individual adds another piece of information to the budget puzzle and a bonding of relationships can occur.

In organizations, it is equally important to hear from as many individuals as is realistically possible. It provides members with the feeling of importance and self worth, and helps to strengthen the feeling of teamwork and commitment to the organization. The additional information from a number of individuals can also make a huge difference on the bottom-line results of the budget.

Many families and organizations develop an *operating budget* for each year that can then be broken down monthly or even weekly. Organizations usually develop a budget for the *fiscal* or financial year which can run concurrently with the calendar year but they can choose any period they like if it is more beneficial, such as July 1st to June 30th or September 1st to August 31st. Families, for the most part operate on a fiscal budget that usually coincides with the calendar year.

Because budgeting is a form of financial planning or management, it is important to consider specific guidelines. Remember to always keep the principles and vision of the group in mind when developing a budget and to invite as many individuals as is realistic and potentially helpful to the budgeting process. The following guidelines for developing a budget were developed in part by Wolf (1999) and Weis and Gantt (2004).

Step 1: *Develop a List of Possible Expenses.* Budgets for most organizations are prepared months in advance of their implementation and it would be wise to do the same thing for a family. This allows time for researching the cost of items and for individuals to share information.

While preparing a list of expenses it is a great idea to look at items on the expense list for the same period of the previous year, and then determine if the items are needed again and if the cost has changed. It is also important to examine any new expenses that might be a part of the new budget year. Expenses should always be projected on the high side in order to absorb any unexpected costs. Families and organizations must also strongly consider including a *contingency/ reserve fund* or process to allow for unforeseen emergencies or for any kind of special expenses in the future, such as a college tuition fund for families or capital outlays for corporations.

Step 2: *Determine Potential Sources of Revenue or Income.* After projecting expense costs for the coming year it's necessary to determine how those costs are going to be handled. The best way to do this is to look at revenue/income from the previous year then determine if that level of finances will change for the coming year. Depending on the expenses projected and any changes in projected revenue/income, some families or organizations may wish to look at new areas of financial development. Income projections are best kept on the low side with flexibility for any potential deficiencies.

After completing the entire budgetary process, if additional revenue or income needs to be considered, a round-table discussions with key group members can be instrumental in determining the best possible alternatives. Family financial planners or corporate financial specialists, committees, and/or consultants can be brought in to assist.

Step 3: *Compare Expense and Income or Revenue Projections.* Following a careful review of projected expenses and projected revenue or income, it's time to evaluate whether or not the projected revenue or income adequately covers and even exceeds projected expenses. If the projected income/revenue adequately exceeds projected expenses, then it may be time to consider inviting those involved in the budgetary process to meet and discuss the acceptance of the budget.

If, on the other hand, after careful review, the expenses exceed income/revenue then one significant way to reduce expenses in the budget can be through a process referred to as *zero-based budgeting*. Zero-based budgeting includes taking line items in the budget to a theoretical zero level where there is no historical base and each line can be considered anew. For instance, telephone costs are something that both families and organizations must deal with. Instead of starting with the basic cost for telephone expenses from the previous year, we start with a theoretical zero base then work on ways to keep the cost of this line item as low as possible for the coming year while maintaining quality.

For instance, changing carriers can bring a significant change in costs, and negotiating for an even lower price with the company being considered can make it even better. Another way is to encourage more e-mail communication and develop a policy that is fair but puts some boundaries on unnecessary long-distance calling. Making these three changes alone can save families hundreds of dollars and organizations thousands—even millions of dollars—in telephone expenses.

Zero-based budgeting provides individuals with the opportunity to examine each expense line of a budget and to make some remarkable changes. It is time consuming, can be controversial, and must be administered wisely. Once the expenses of a budget are processed down to a realistic figure, and the expenses still outweigh the income/revenue, then it is time to look for additional income/revenue opportunities as mentioned in Step 2.

Step 4: *Setting Activity and Project Priorities.* Once everything is done to reduce projected expenses and to develop realistic income/revenue opportunities and a budget still doesn't balance, then it may be time to determine priorities and make some hard decisions. Group members may then have to ask each other the following questions.

1. Which activities or projects are central to the purpose and vision of our group?
2. Which activities or projects are costing more than they're worth?
3. Which activities or projects can be altered or eliminated without endangering the overall success of our group?

These are hard questions to ask, but are necessary to develop priorities and to move forward with financial soundness.

Step 5: *Adjust and Balance the Budget.* Once all of the expenses and all of the income/revenue have been carefully considered and priorities set, then it is time to write the figures on a budget sheet with expenses on one side and income/revenue on the other, and be sure that the totals balance. Remember to place a reasonable and realistic figure in the contingency/reserve fund for unforeseen expenses and growth or new ventures.

Because the budget has been developed with projected expectations on the high side for expenses and on the low side for income/revenue, then it is conceivable that there may money "left over" and the budget is out of balance. If this occurs, the projected extra amount can be added to the contingency/reserve line for reasons mentioned above.

> You cannot keep out of trouble
> by spending more than your income.
> —Abraham Lincoln

Step 6: *Time for Budget Approval.* Although families operate with different parameters than organizations and businesses, it's important for the leaders of a family to share the knowledge of a proposed budget and to understand the financial parameters in which the family is operating. Sharing a completed draft of a proposed budget with other family members should be considered but may not be realistic, depending on variables such as age and "need to know." If other members of a family are invited to review the draft of the budget, they should be encouraged to ask questions and make suggestions. Remember, a budget is a projection, and reality can be quite different; if the information is shared, members should be better able to handle shifts from projection to reality.

Organizations and businesses operate with a different mind-set, of course, and it will depend on such documents as by-laws, constitution, and policy as to how a budget is approved. Generally, the budget is developed by key financial planners with the help of those in the trenches. Usually it is first approved by a committee, often a committee of the board of directors prior to going to a full board for complete approval. At each stage of the approval process, questions should be encouraged and suggestions invited and genuinely considered.

Step 7: *Monitoring and Amending Effectively.* Again, families operate within different boundaries than organizations and businesses but once a budget has been developed and accepted, it should be monitored carefully. Developing an effective budget is one thing, but implementing budgets successfully is another and takes just as much attention as the planning phase if not more.

Family leaders need to monitor the budget on a weekly and monthly basis to be sure that the expense and income sides are working according to plan. Key organizational staff and/or board members are selected to carefully monitor organizational budgets and to report to specified groups as to the operational success of a budget.

It is not uncommon for groups to amend budgets within a budgetary year when necessary. Usually, this happens when there are unforeseen expenses but it can also occur when income/revenue exceeds projections. However, if a budget has been carefully prepared, it may only need one or two revisions a year if any. Making no more than one or two revisions a year provides some flexibility without taking it to extremes.

Input is integral for revised budgets just as it is for an original budget. Family leaders can make these revisions easily and without a great deal of fanfare. Organizations, on the other hand often have restrictions, guidelines, and policies as to the number of revisions that can be made, the types of revisions, and the process for implementing the revisions including the policy regarding officially approving the revised budget.

Another important consideration in the budgetary process for both organizations and families is the concept of *cash flow* which is projecting a family or an organizations income and expenses on a month-to-month basis as well as an annual basis. During certain months and certain seasons, expenses may be higher or lower than usual and likewise for income/revenue. Families and organizations must be prepared for these potential circumstances and be certain that income/revenue is adequate to meet the expenses for each month. One way to do this is to have an adequate *contingency fund* that could be used for various situations and hopefully refunded later on. Another way is to maintain good relationships with lending institutions and be as aware as possible of low- or no-interest loans.

Group leaders should also consider the concept of *stewardship*, which implies managing one's own resources as well as maintaining a respectable regard for the rights and resources of others. Taking the role of stewardship seriously would mean that family and organizational leaders should not only consider their own group's well being when making plans for using resources but also to consider the well being of others. This can sometimes seem like a daunting task because the world is competitive but good group leaders can be competitive and still respect the well being of other individuals and groups by maintaining integrity and fairness in all transactions.

A great way to help instill the concept of stewardship in group members is by sharing resources such as time, expertise, energy, and money with youth, human service, or other nonprofit organizations. This provides support to those organizations and instills pride and a sense of bonding to group members as well. This sense of stewardship needs to be shared with all group members and individuals should be encouraged to continue what can become a traditional characteristic of the group.

> The one principle that surrounds everything else is that of stewardship; that we are the managers of everything that God has given us.
>
> —Larry Burkett

A strong budget is almost always essential for the success of any work group or family.

Which of the budgeting steps mentioned in this section can help make your budget better (work group or family)?

_____
_____
_____
_____
_____
_____
_____
_____

Are you already implementing the concept of *stewardship* with your group or family? If not, how can you initiate this concept in the future?

_____
_____
_____
_____
_____
_____
_____

Achieving a Balanced Life

Leaders in families and organizations often feel pulled in many different directions. It is important for each of us to do all that we can to maintain a *balanced life* so that we can reach for our goals and help others reach for their goals while keeping ourselves refreshed for all that we wish to do in life.

> On the tightrope of life, only one thing allows us to move forward, and that one thing is balance. Without balance we fall into chaos, we fall behind, we miss out on what true choices we have in life.
>
> —Laura Kangas

Too often we spend so much time concentrating on goals that we don't take the time to enjoy life and replenish ourselves. It's amazing how much more productive and creative we can be when we are relaxed.

Maintaining a balanced approach to life allows us the opportunity to work toward our goals with a smile on our face and a skip in our walk. A balanced life is especially important for leaders in families and organizations because of the high expectations on their shoulders and because they need to set examples and help with guidelines for others to lead a balanced life as well. The 7 keys below should help all members of a group stay focused on the group's purpose while engaging in other important aspects of life.

1. ***Set and check priorities in light of your overall purpose in life.*** The first key to maintaining a balanced life is to remember to focus on the family or organization's mission and vision while realizing that all members of the group need to feel refreshed and reenergized, and that they need to experience and participate in many other facets of life. At the same time group

members need to hold tight to the principles and values that are a part of the group's culture.

The mission, vision, and guiding principles of the group are interconnected and, while keeping focused on these three areas is critical, it is equally important that group members experience and participate in activities that refresh and inspire them to stay focused like the activities we will present below. A leader's job is to help group members stay focused on the group's purpose, and to feel inspired and refreshed enough to be able to do that.

2. ***Keep stressors under control.*** Stress in life is inevitable and a certain amount of stress is important because it motivates us to reach certain goals and meet certain needs. As a matter of fact, some people seem to thrive on stress. We often experience stress when we are faced with or perceive dangerous or uncomfortable circumstances.

Stress activates our *sympathetic nervous system* which has an affect on our heart, muscles, and other parts of our body. Stress hormones flow to nearly all areas of our body so that our body can be aroused to meet the demands of the situation. Once the demands are met, stress levels typically subside and we usually return to a more normal state. But sometimes threats or perceived threats or uncomfortable situations don't subside and our body stays on constant alert. Or sometimes there are so many threats or perceived threats that we never seem to go off alert. This can lead to high blood pressure, heart disease, depression, anxiety, headaches, and other diseases associated with our immune system. Stress can tear at the very fiber that holds the family unit together. In organizations, it can result in low productivity and morale, absenteeism, substance abuse, high turnovers, and even accidents (Ivancevich and Matteson, 1980).

Stress can come from all directions; changes in our personal lives, good or bad, can create stress. For instance, even though a wedding is generally considered a happy time, it is also stressful because of the planning and changes in life style. Other stress factors in an individual's personal life can include divorce or separation, child birth, death of a close relative or friend, or a move to another part of the country. We also experience stress with our organizational lives in the form of working with people with whom we are not comfortable, feeling pressured to succeed, and feeling overwhelmed with the work load and unappreciated for our part in the overall operation of the organization.

> The older I grow, the more clearly I perceive
> the dignity and beauty of simplicity
> in thought, conduct and speech;
> a desire to simplify all that is complicated
> and to treat everything with the greatest
> naturalness and clarity.
>
> —Pope John XXIII

A leader needs to understand how to handle personal stress effectively before a leader can help others in the group. The following areas of stress management can lead to a healthier, happier leader and offer opportunities to share these processes for stress reduction with others:

- *Set priorities according to values.* Stress is sometimes the result of spending too much time on issues that are of little value and not enough time on areas of greater value. Too often we follow routines that we believe are necessary for success but lead to a stressful life because we fail to slow down and understand what's really important. So take time to assess what really is important in life and start making time for those priorities. As a leader, let group members know that the mission of the group is very high in value but other priorities in life are just as important.

- *Develop support systems.* One of the most important areas of stress management is sharing thoughts and feelings with appropriate individuals. In families, friends and other family members should be considered first, but sometimes professionals can be helpful with certain individual, marital, and family concerns. In organizations, formal and informal colleague support groups and peer counseling can be very helpful in stress reduction, and appropriate professional colleagues should also be considered, just as in families.

- *Create a healthy environment.* Providing an environment where individuals feel important and where they have a satisfying level of control with their environment is critical in managing stress. People under stress whether at home or at work also need opportunities to release stress through social, cultural, and recreational activities. Organizing trips to museums, zoos, or theme parks, kayaking on the bay, or participating in softball leagues can pull us away from daily grinds and transport us to happier experiences

> It is not stress that kills us,
> it is our reaction to it.
>
> —Hans Selye

Other ways to handle stress include exercise, healthy diets, hobbies, music, time management, yoga, massage, tai chi, meditation, prayer, and community service; a few of these will be discussed later in this section. Norman Vincent Peale once said that "(People) have become so tense and nervous that it's been years since I've seen anyone fall asleep in church . . . and that's a sad situation!"

3. *Cultivate and maintain healthy relationships.* Developing and maintaining close relationships throughout life is essential for a healthy, balanced person. Some might say that it is one of the most important factors in leading to a balanced life because of the extraordinary need all of us have for connecting with others and avoiding loneliness.

> The supreme happiness in life is
> the conviction that we are loved.
>
> —Victor Hugo

Like all living forms we need stimulation and one of the best ways to engage in stimulation is through human contact.

We engage in *intellectual stimulation* by discussing our ideas with others by going to school, church, museums, and other venues where social interaction can occur. We share our thoughts and listen to others share theirs and develop our attitudes, knowledge base, and belief system in the process. We also need *physical stimulation*. Holding and shaking hands, patting each other on the back, and looking at and being seen by others are all important for our well being. *Emotional stimulation* is also important. Being able to express our feelings through smiles, laughter, and tears, and to experience those same feelings from others can be the basis of bonding for friendships, work relationships, and families (DeVito, 2001).

Healthy relationships are relationships that have been nurtured and that seem to thrive for long periods of time. There is a sense of well being and stability in healthy relationships and a sense that individuals in the relationship add to the quality of life for each other. Good relationships don't develop by accident and the areas discussed below can work together to create and sustain us through life's pathways (Relationship-Helps-And-Advice.com):

- *Mutual Respect.* Having a healthy respect for the thoughts and feelings of another is important, even when some of those thoughts and feelings can differ significantly from our own. Mutual respect also implies that the individuals are generally comfortable with each other's decision-making processes.

- *Trust.* Being able to count on another and to be counted on is essential for the development of trust. Trust is something that is earned through word *and* deed. We need to feel safe, physically and emotionally, before we can have trust in one another.

- *Support.* Individuals in healthy relationships support and nurture each other always, but particularly in times of difficulty and stress. Support can come in the form of emotional support, physical support, mental support, spiritual support, and financial support; it is important to know that someone is there to help when help is needed most.

- *Honesty.* Sharing the truth with another—believing in the other person—is a significant requirement for developing healthy relationships. Being true to yourself and to the other person is essential in developing strong, lasting bonds.

- *Fairness.* Understanding the person and compromising and collaborating with them in all aspects will lead to a stronger relationship based on each person carrying an agreed upon and accepted share of the load. Individuals in solid relationships have a good understanding of expectations and limitations. Good relationships have a win/win foundation where each person experiences a sense of fairness.

- *Separate Identities.* Too often in relationships we believe the other person should be just like us; sharing the same beliefs and attitudes and behaving in a certain fashion. And sometimes we believe this so fully that we stretch ourselves to become more like the other person. In fact, expecting someone to change or trying to change for someone else can put a lot of stress on a relationship. Appreciating oneself and others for who they are and their differences can be enriching for many relationships.

- *Good Communication.* Good communication involves *active listening* and *understanding.* Active listening involves hearing what an individual has to say, then restating it to see if you understood what they said in the first place. This response provides the other person an opportunity to clarify her/his intended meaning. Once there is an understanding of one issue, then the discussion can more safely move on to another issue.

- *Commitment.* Having a strong belief in another person or a commitment to the relationship is one of the most important considerations in a relationship (Weis and Gantt, 2004). Relationships with a commitment can endure long and difficult circumstances and still come out on top.

Developing closeness with others is critical for healthy and successful relationships. In the book, *The Seven Levels of Intimacy: The Art of Loving and the Joy of Being Loved,* Matthew Kelly describes the four areas of life in which we need to develop closeness with others—emotional, intellectual, spiritual, and physical—and then expertly describes ways to develop that closeness (2005). We encourage you to check out this exceptional reading.

Healthy relationships in any group are vitally important and make the difference between a successful group and one in constant turmoil. Understanding and practicing key aspects of healthy relationships will help family and organizational leaders to develop good relationships, become role models for group members, and provide guidance for others to follow.

> *Eighty percent of life's satisfaction comes from meaningful relationships.*
> —Brian Tracy

4. **Manage time in light of priorities (not in 24 hour increments).** Too often we feel overwhelmed with life's responsibilities and the limited time to fulfill them. We are accustomed to progressing through each day completing tasks and running around in a whirlwind, and then feeling that we really didn't accomplish very much. We feel that we have placed much too much emphasis on things that aren't important and not enough emphasis on things that are. In fact, we have as much time as anyone else; it is all a matter of how deciding how to spend our time, and then just doing that.

One key to managing time effectively is to realize that we have choices in nearly every facet of our lives about how we manage one of the most important resources we have, our time. We tend to believe we are slaves to time when the truth is that we have chosen the way we spend time. As a matter of fact, time is one of our most valuable resources and we need to spend it wisely; it is limited, yes, but it is our choice how we spend it. Following the three guidelines discussed below can provide insight and support for managing time according to your choices.

- *Prioritize your time according to what you value.* The most important step in managing your time effectively is to realize that you need to manage your time around what is really important to you and not around the clock. You first must determine what the most important aspects of your life are at home and at work, then prioritize your time around these. The first thing you need to do is to look inside yourself and decide what expectations you have of yourself and what your family, friends, and community expect from you. Talk with family members and friends about expectations and try and decide what is realistic and effective for everyone. Next, you need to do the same thing at work. Review the expectations you have of yourself and develop an understanding of the importance of these expectations. Then you may wish to brain storm with colleagues and with your supervisor(s) and discuss their expectations. Having clear expectations is critical in all of life and essential in helping prioritize our time.

> The key is not to prioritize what's on your schedule, but to schedule your priorities.
>
> —Stephen Covey

- *Organize your time around your values.* Divide your time up into broad areas and categories (Raffoni, 2006). Two major areas could be home and work. Time at home could then be divided up into categories such as family time, home improvement, community service, shopping, and just relaxing. Time at work could be divided into supervision, production, meetings, communication, and personnel enrichment. Categories can be added or subtracted, of course, depending on the family or the organization. After you've selected your categories in each area, then decide on the approximate percentage of time you are spending on each category. After careful consideration, estimate the approximate amount of time you would like to spend in each category. Study these time calculations for accuracy with someone you trust and are close to at home and at work, then make note of your calculations. How you spend your time should be determined by what you value and prioritized accordingly.

- *Manage your time and life around your values.* Understanding what you value and organizing your life around those values is important. But if you don't implement that plan it is all for naught. Motivate yourself to keep track of your time using a journal and compare your results with your plan. If your plan seems unrealistic, it may need to be adjusted but be careful to adjust it in line with your priorities. The more disciplined you are at first, the better. New systems or processes often seem awkward at first use and sometimes we just need to work through those awkward situations for great results down the road.

> Life isn't about finding yourself.
> Life is about creating yourself.
>
> —Author Unknown

5. ***Participate in and encourage civic engagement.*** Encouraging family and organizational members to become more actively involved in civic matters provides leaders with opportunities to make a difference in their communities. This is true of ordinary day-to-day events as well as for situations that compel us to take a stand on various issues.

   One example of how leaders can make a difference at home and at work could be the issue of smoking. Countless studies have proven beyond a doubt that smoking and the breathing of second-hand smoke is extremely hazardous to one's health. Some communities and some states have organized campaigns to ban smoking from public and private places. Banning smoking can be controversial and complicated. Many people still smoke in spite of the known dangers, and many still smoke around children in spite of the known perils of second-hand smoke. Exposure to passive smoke can cause asthma, bronchitis, and pneumonia and it is especially dangerous to children and pregnant women.

   Encouraging those you live with and work with to get involved in effective campaigns to limit smoking areas can be a great way to address an important social and health issue while developing a bonding experience for those involved with the effort. A "grass roots" effort at home and at work or participating in existing grass roots efforts can help further develop the foundation of successful families and organizations. (It is important to note that smoking is still generally legal and it is important to respect the rights of smokers who are smoking within legal parameters.)

   Encouraging those at home and at work who are eligible to vote in local and national elections is yet another way to offer individuals the opportunity to make a difference and to feel that they are an important part of a team that cares about the way communities and issues are organized and addressed.

6. ***Make a difference in the lives of others.*** Making a difference in the life of someone else through involvement at school, in a community service organization, or through a place of worship is one of the greatest ways to realize happiness and develop a more balanced life. Mentoring a child through the Big Brothers/Big Sisters program, coaching a team in a YMCA flag football league, or ministering to the elderly and disabled in a nursing home can make all the difference in someone's life as well as providing you with one of the greatest feelings imaginable. Make the time to explore your community needs through contact with your local United Way agency,

school systems, organization of churches, or Chamber of Commerce to find out what needs exist in your community and to see where your knowledge and skills can be of service. Leaders who volunteer their time for community needs make a difference for the sake of making a difference, but they also serve as role models for family and organizational members. An even stronger statement can be made by leaders who not only give of their time and talents, but also encourages those around them to make a difference as well.

The most important reason to volunteer your time is to make a difference in at least one other person's life. But studies and reports indicate that those who do volunteer have higher self images than those who do not, and on the average live longer, healthier lives. So it's a win/win for all concerned.

> Life's most urgent question is: what are you doing for others?
>
> —Martin Luther King, Jr.

7. **Take care of yourself.** Too often leaders are so busy with organizing and producing results that they don't take the time to take care of themselves. Boldly put, this is a selfish attitude. If you don't take care of yourself, you'll reach your limits too soon and too often, and deprive others of the value of your presence.

The concept of *wellness* means to take responsibility for your own health by learning ways to stay healthy, initiating healthy habits and excluding harmful ones, and responding to your body's warning signals by seeing a health care provider. Keeping your body strong and well nourished helps you to avoid injury or disease. Keeping your mind alert and your spirits high can also help to reduce stress, anxiety, and other health complications (*Wellness In Your Life*, 2005). Taking care of yourself helps you to be a better leader at home and at work. The following areas are health factors that you can control. Always check with a health care professional prior to initiating the following recommendations:

- *Nutrition:* Living well begins with eating well. Before adjusting your diet you need to have an understanding of what healthy eating is and is not. You also need to understand that changes in eating habits don't work unless there is a change in mindset or life style that fits with a healthier diet. Some target areas for change can include getting less dietary fat by choosing low or non-fat dairy products and by eating more fish, poultry, vegetables, and fruits and less meats, butter, and animal fats. Another target area is reducing sugar intake by cutting back on sweets in cereals, sodas, and pastries, and reducing sodium intake by choosing unsalted or lightly salted snacks, processed foods, and condiments. It is also important to include more fiber in your diet by choosing whole grain breads, cereals, fruits, and vegetables. If you think you need to lose or gain weight, check with a nutritionist and dietitian or health care provider in your community. For a more complete understanding of healthy diets contact the American Dietetic Association at 800-877-1600 or *www.eatright.org* or contact the Food and Nutrition Information Center (*fnic.nal.usda.gov*)

- *Exercise:* Regular physical activity and exercise helps to prevent heart disease, stroke, diabetes, obesity, and osteoporosis. Additionally, it helps to manage high blood pressure and cholesterol (Just Move! American Heart Association, 2003). Individuals who exercise on a regular basis tend to feel better, sleep better, and have less stress. Activities to consider include brisk walking, bicycling, jogging, swimming, roller blading, racquetball, basketball. and tennis. If you are not currently involved with exercising, start slowly with 5 to 10 minute intervals until you can build up to 30 minutes a day most days of the week. You can also add weight lifting to build muscle strength. Be sure to stretch before and after your workouts. Before you begin an exercise program, consider your general health and physical capabilities along with your interests. You may wish to get the advice of fitness experts and to include family and friends in your routines when possible. Be certain you have the best equipment, shoes, and clothing as possible and stay hydrated at all times. Starting and stopping won't help; you need to make a commitment and be as consistent as possible. Remember, always check with a health care professional prior to initiating physical activity and exercise, and monitor your progress with your health care professional.

> Movement is a medicine for creating change in a person's physical, emotional, and mental states.
>
> —Carol Welch

- *Travel:* Traveling can be one of the best "attitude adjustments" and a way to learn about other areas, cultures, people, and yourself. Getting away from it all can provide breaks from the monotony of daily activities at home and at work, and provide a world of adventure and/or relaxation. Traveling is a way to reconnect with friends and family and provide lasting memories for all involved. It is another way to keep yourself refreshed so you can be the best version of yourself possible.

- *Spirituality:* Spiritual individuals are often hopeful and enthusiastic. They are generally optimistic that things will work out for the best and often have a plan and a willingness to work toward positive results for all involved. Spiritual individuals are filled with emotions and a belief system in which good is stronger than evil. They believe we only need to focus on the good in ourselves and others to generate successful outcomes. Connecting spirituality to a religion can provide strength and resolve. Most studies indicate that people associated with religion are generally happier and healthier. Helping others find and practice their spiritual selves is a role that good leaders should welcome and practice.

> The foundations of a person are not in matter but in spirit.
>
> —Ralph Waldo Emerson

- *Rest:* For healthy minds and hearts it is generally suggested that we experience "down time" each and every day and strive for between 7 to 8 hours of sleep nightly. Energy is restored during rest and sleep so that we can continue with valued activities. We all need to develop "protected times" when we can take a break or get some sleep. Protected times can be when we are just relaxing or recreating with friends or family. Recreation takes many different forms, of course, but the most important ones are those you enjoy and make you feel rejuvenated. Yoga, tai chi, prayer, and meditative activities all restore energy and rejuvenate our thought processes while helping our bodies become less stressed. Getting enough sleep can be helped by cutting down on caffeine, eating less especially later in the evenings, and cutting out tobacco because nicotine is a stimulant that can lead to frequent awakenings. Individuals with a consistent exercise routine, who keep sleeping areas cool and dark, and who incorporate a fan or white-noise machine to block out noises tend to sleep better (*www.calumet.purdue.edu*).

- *Other Lifestyle Changes:* Taking good care of yourself sometimes means changes in lifestyle. For example, limit alcohol consumption or stop drinking altogether. Overuse of alcohol can result in heart and liver problems and damage to the brain. Try to avoid people and situations that encourage drinking to excess. NEVER drink and drive, if you are pregnant, or if you are a recovering alcoholic. Drinking alone or drinking to escape the pressures of life can lead to alcohol dependency; be aware of this possibility and see a health care professional for assistance. Another lifestyle change to take better care of yourself is to stop smoking and avoid areas where there is environmental tobacco smoke (ETS), also known as second-hand smoke. Smoking and environmental smoke can lead to heart, lung, and respiratory diseases. One of the hardest things to do is to quit smoking because of the strong physiological and psychological addiction associated with it, but it is also one of the most important things a smoker can do. There are lots of successful ways a health care provider or local health department can help someone with who is interested in stopping smoking.

Maintaining a balanced lifestyle can be tricky but it's a way to maintain success for yourself in all realms of life. Keeping yourself refreshed and healthy is a great way to be a successful leader at home and at work, and it also sets a good example for others to follow. Leaders need to always be aware that a balanced life is essential for them and those around them and to integrate processes to reach a balanced life for all concerned.

> Each second you can be reborn.
> Each second there can be
> a new beginning.
> It is a choice.
> It is your choice.
>
> —Clearwater

How balanced is your life, at present?

_____
_____
_____
_____
_____
_____
_____
_____
_____

What changes do you need to make to make for it to be more balanced?

_____
_____
_____
_____
_____
_____
_____
_____
_____

What are you willing to do to make those changes? What is needed for you to commit to a more balanced life at work and at home?

_____
_____
_____
_____
_____
_____
_____

What about other group and family members? How balanced are their lives and how can you assist them?

_____
_____
_____
_____
_____
_____
_____
_____

Understanding and Developing Human Relations Competencies

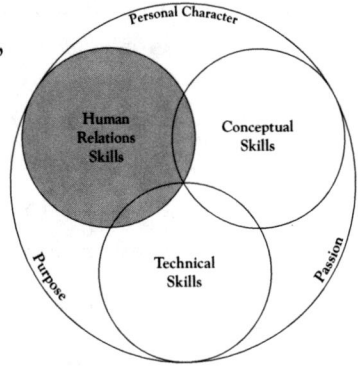

Once a vision is realized and a plan is developed, it's time to share that plan effectively with others. Human relation skills are thought by many to be among the most important competency areas in life. A number of human relation competencies are important to apply at home and work, and include motivation, conflict management, teamwork, and valuing diversity.

Creating a Motivational Environment

Motivation is the initiative and energy to meet goals and to make a difference in your life as well as the lives of others. We are motivated by our needs and by what we value. It is a leader's responsibility to help address the needs and values of others in working toward the goals of the family and/or organization. Before motivational processes can be implemented properly, a foundation of trust needs to be developed between the leader and members of the group. It is also important for a leader to understand that individuals are motivated in different ways and a *motivational environment* can be created so that numerous opportunities exist for individuals to be inspired and motivated.

First, we'll look at the building blocks essential for establishing a foundation of trust in order for a motivational environment to work:

1. **Integrity:** A leader of any organization must be someone that can be trusted and counted on for important matters. They must be perceived as someone who will be responsible for the well being of all individuals and of the overall purpose of the group. Leading with integrity means standing up for the values of the group and maintaining those values and a high level of ethical standards even in turbulent times.

2. **Clear Goals and Purpose:** A good leader helps to develop clear and shared expectations for individuals in order to reach toward the goals and overall

purpose of the group. Determining what the group is all about and sharing in goal setting and achievement is a bonding experience and leaders need to articulate the process clearly and often and support individuals in the process.

3. **Emphasis on Needs and Values:** Understanding individual needs and values and how those needs and values fit with the overall purpose of the group are essential in establishing a motivational environment. Individual and group values should be discussed and encouraged. We'll take a closer look at individual needs and how they fit into the scheme of things later in this section.

4. **Concern:** One of the most important concepts that a leader in a business, organization, or a family should convey to others is that there is *genuine* concern on the part of the leader for group members. When group members believe that a leader has their best interests in mind, they are much more likely to develop a bond with that person and more likely to trust the direction the organization is heading.

> People don't care how much you know until they know how much you care.
> —John C. Maxwell

5. **Commitment:** Good leaders maintain a high level of commitment to the overall purpose of the organization or family, and are great models of holding that purpose in high esteem. Because of that high level of commitment they are also able to keep group members more focused on the activities and goals of the group.

Group leaders are not perfect individuals and like anyone else make mistakes and occasionally stray from their values and goals. Whenever this happens, she/he must be able to admit to mistakes and make genuine and effective changes to regain the trust of others and to stay on track for the future.

> *I don't measure a man's success by how high he climbs but how high he bounces when he hits the bottom.*
>
> —General George S. Patton

When group leader establishes a foundation of trust with group members, then a *motivational environment* is more likely to be created. Although there are numerous motivational concepts that can be used to inspire others, we will look at two that are held in high regard by many in the leadership/motivational field. In his book, *Developing the Leader Within You*, John Maxwell (1993) identifies five different ways that people feel motivated:

- *Significant Contributions.* Individuals are much more likely to be inspired if they feel like their efforts are appreciated and are making a positive difference. They need to feel as if what they are doing will have a lasting impact and that it will contribute toward the group's goals.

- *Goal Participation.* Involving others in determining the goals and mission of an organization allows them the opportunity to feel as if they have had a say in the development of the goals, which can lead to a higher level of ownership. Setting goals together also creates the opportunity for more diversity in the goal-setting process.

- *Positive Dissatisfaction.* Dissatisfaction in almost any part of life can lead to wanting to change things. Dissatisfied people are much more likely to have the energy and will to change a situation and, with positive guidance, dissatisfaction can be turned into new ideas and directions for change.

- *Recognition.* People generally feel motivated through personal accomplishments but most individuals like to be appreciated for the work they do. Often that appreciation can be expressed through personal thanks and congratulations, but sometimes it needs to be expressed more formally.

- *Clear Expectations.* Understanding what is expected of you is extremely important in relationships at home and at work. Discussing tasks and developing guidelines to achieve those tasks are essential. Enabling individuals to work toward those tasks with effective monitoring allows them some control in what they are accomplishing.

When leaders establish processes that allow individuals to work together to develop goals, to understand what is expected of them, and that offer encouragement for their efforts, an *energetic motivational environment* emerges.

> When we are motivated by goals
> that have deep meaning,
> by dreams that need completion,
> by pure love that needs expressing,
> then we truly live life.
>
> —Greg Anderson

Another motivational concept was developed by Abraham Maslow (1943) that still serves as a foundation for understanding human needs today. Maslow's concept is referred to as the Hierarchy of Needs Theory in which he identified five basic areas of needs; physiological needs, safety needs, affiliation needs, esteem needs, and the need to become self actualized:

- *Physiological Needs.* Our most basic needs are for food, water, sleep, and sensory gratification. Good leaders recognize the significance of this and do everything possible to create a supportive environment so that those who have been entrusted to them can connect with these needs. Family members need to feel that their parents/leaders are doing everything possible to make them comfortable in these areas, and employees must believe that their leaders are doing everything possible to offer fair and effective compensation for their efforts.

- *Safety and Protection.* Another important basic need for individuals is to feel that their home and work environment are relatively free from danger and that leaders are constantly evaluating the home and work environment to make them as safe as possible. Maintaining a safe home in a safe neighborhood allows family members to feel protected and able to meet other challenges in life; the same is true for a safe work environment. Knowing that safety is of the utmost importance is comforting and encourages individuals to move forward in addressing other areas.

- *Affiliation.* One of the most important needs that we all have is the desire to join with others in the development of a family or to complete a task at work. The feeling of being cared for by someone and of caring for that other person in various environments is one of the strongest needs. Leaders of families must help family members feel cared for and loved, and organizational leaders must ensure that employees feel that they are a significant part of the team.

- *Self-Esteem.* Individuals and groups typically feel better about themselves when there is a sense of achievement. This can result in internal satisfaction when people feel a sense of accomplishment and success and know that they are counted on. Or, it can result in external satisfaction in the form of visible rewards such as a pat on the back, a thank you, or an allowance or salary increase (Weis & Gantt, 2004).

- *Self-Actualization.* Maslow believed that most people strive to become everything they are capable of becoming, and once they have reached a very high standard in various areas, they then have the desire to help others reach their goals and dreams as well. Leaders in families and organizations have the opportunity to encourage those who have been successful in various areas to assist others in reaching their goals and dreams.

Throughout his writings, Maslow indicated that it was important for individuals to satisfy their basic needs such as food, water. and shelter before attempting to satisfy very important but more abstract needs such as the need for affiliation or self-esteem. An organizational leader who embraces Maslow's concept can create a *motivational environment* that allows individuals to meet needs on all different levels. A family leader can provide opportunities for individuals to share in reaching basic needs and to feel as if they are valued contributors to the well being of the family; thereby developing healthy self-esteem.

Meeting our needs and goals and doing what we believe to be important and fulfilling is motivational, and good leaders understand the complexities of what motivates others and strive to create the most effective *motivational environment* possible. *Motivational environments* are supportive and offer a myriad of ways to help us to find and reach toward our purpose in life.

Reflection & Application

Each of us is motivated in different ways.

What are some of the areas you can change to create a more motivational environment for yourself?

_____
_____
_____
_____
_____
_____
_____

What about creating a "motivational environment" for those in your family/organization? What would it "look" like?

_____
_____
_____
_____
_____
_____
_____
_____

Managing Conflict

Conflict is a normal part of life and can lead to positive outcomes when handled effectively. Conflict often occurs when two or more parties disagree with each other regarding interests, ideas, goals, behavior, beliefs, or the use of resources and express that disagreement in some way.

Gone unchecked, conflict can lead to negative thoughts and feelings, and even actions. Individuals involved in a disagreement sometimes feel defensive of their position and remain guarded toward the other individual(s) involved in the disagreement. This defensiveness in a family or organization tends to deplete energy and pull time and resources away from other important areas in which the group is involved.

Managing conflict is far from easy but essential for families and organizations to work together successfully. There are a number of *unproductive conflict strategies* that need to be avoided. For instance, physical and/or mental *avoidance* can leave a situation unresolved and lead to depletion of energy and effectiveness. *Non-negotiation* is an unproductive strategy where one of the parties refuses to discuss a conflict. *Steamrolling* is where one of the parties refuses to even listen to the other's side and keeps hammering at their own points of view until the other person gives in or leaves the group (De Vito, 2002). And there are lots of other demeaning, unproductive, unsuccessful ways to handle conflict that need to be carefully avoided.

On the positive side, when a conflict arises, it provides individuals with the opportunity to face the problem head on and to work together toward managing it. One model of conflict resolution that deals with it effectively involves the following steps (DeVito, 2002):

- *Define the issue.* One of the most important steps in managing conflict is defining what the issue is about. Many times conflict can arise simply because the parties involved have a misunderstanding of expectations or actions, so it is important for all parties to be very specific with any and all concerns. Asking questions and confirming the other person's interpretation of the issue and clearly stating your own is a significant move toward resolving concerns.

- *Examine possible solutions.* The most successful solution is one that leads to a win/win for all parties concerned. In other words, each party feels as if their concerns have been addressed. A win/lose solution could result in immediate and even long-term resentment and conflict. When weighing the best solution, discuss the ups and downs of each solution for everyone involved and arrive at an equitable arrangement for all.

> True peace is not merely the absence of tension; it is the presence of justice.
>
> —Martin Luther King, Jr.

- *Test the solution.* Once a solution has been selected, test it out mentally to see how it feels for now and for the future. Examine as many possible consequences as possible. Each party should be involved in this exercise. Next, implement your solution and if it doesn't feel right to those involved, go to the next plan.

- *Evaluate the solution.* Once you have decided on the solution and have tried it out in practice, you'll need to get together and discuss whether the solution chosen has actually helped in resolving the conflict. Monitoring the progress of a solution is critical and needs to involve all parties. Do the positives outweigh the negatives?

- *Accept or reject the solution.* If the solution feels right to all parties then it becomes a more permanent part of operation. If there are still concerns, you can modify the solution or go back to the original conflict, examine it more closely to see if yet another solution should be put into effect, and begin again.

There is another great model for conflict management that involves choosing from five options when faced with a conflict: *avoiding, accommodating, competing, compromising,* or *collaborating* (Borisoff and Victor, 1998). And while each of the options has its place, choosing one of the first four options may allow some conflicts to remain unresolved.

- *Avoiding.* Avoidance can actually be a very strong style of managing conflict if there is some risk of harm involved; in other situations, avoidance has a tendency to allow conflicts grow if not addressed. Avoidance rarely results in conflict resolution and generally leaves all parties unsatisfied. A residual effect can occur if the conflict is never adequately managed and relationships can be damaged and goals not reached.

- *Accommodating.* If one of the parties involved in a conflict is insistent on a certain avenue in addressing an issue and that avenue is not greatly unacceptable to other parties involved, then accommodating an individual by giving in can be effective. However, once one individual is accommodated for by another, the latter can sometimes be perceived as easily taken advantage of, so accommodation should be considered carefully.

- *Competing.* When information provided to the group indicates one option is clearly beneficial over another, then that option may need to be strongly encouraged as the group's choice. But when there is not a clear-cut direction for an issue, this option can lead to disillusionment and dissatisfaction on the part of group members thus leading to a disappointing environment. This option tends to discourage open and honest communication.

- *Compromising.* When there is not a strong, clear-cut direction a group should choose, then sometimes it may be acceptable to allow all parties involved to give up some ground to reach a decision on an issue. The down side of this style is that all individuals involved may feel somewhat disappointed for giving in.

- *Collaborating.* When a group reaches a direction that makes sense to all involved, then satisfaction is enhanced throughout. The collaborating approach to address an issue or conflict focuses on the best way to manage the issue and not on individual positions. This process generally takes a good deal more time and energy, but results in a direction that can be readily embraced and group members that feel empowered and more likely to enthusiastically participate in conflict management in the future. The collaborating style of conflict management is the most desirable style for most situations.

Good leaders help group members learn positive ways to manage conflict and practice those methods for others to see. In addition to the process mentioned above, it is also a good idea to approach conflict management with a *win/win* mindset like the following three ideas (Weis and Gantt, 2004):

- *Look at the conflict from the other person's point of view.* Understanding the other person's point of view provides you with more information and helps the other person see that you are attempting to be fair.

- *Use "active listening" to hear and understand the other person's viewpoints.* Carefully verify what the other person is saying and ask pertinent questions.

- *Consider assistance from principled negotiators.* Sometimes the conflict may seem so monumental that solutions should be sought from individuals valued and trusted by all parties involved in the conflict.

Managing conflict is far from easy, but once a group has the information and guidance they need to address conflict positively, then it's a matter of practicing the successful processes over and over again until it becomes a part of group culture.

> The most important single ingredient in the formula of success is knowing how to get along with people.
> —Theodore Roosevelt

Reflection & Application

Think about a recent conflict that occurred in your family or organization.

How was it managed?

_____
_____
_____
_____
_____
_____
_____
_____

What ideas/concepts listed in this section could have been helpful?

_____
_____
_____
_____
_____
_____
_____
_____

Which of the ideas/concepts discussed in this section do you plan to use in the future?

Building Great Teams

Encouraging others to work together can be challenging especially in a culture that emphasizes competition and being the best. But for families and organizations to work toward their common goals, they must be supportive and understanding and realize that it is much more effective to plan and reach goals cooperatively. There are plenty of examples in business, sports, and families of great teams, but to find a great example of teamwork, you only have to look out the window.

Nature observers discovered sometime ago that "geese" work exceptionally well together in flying south in the spring and back north in the summer (Weis and Gantt, 2004):

- By flapping its wings, each bird provides uplift for the bird following and by flying in the V formation it helps to almost double the distance that a single bird can fly.

- Soon after a bird drops out of formation it realizes the significant drag and resistance of flying alone and quickly rejoins the flock.

- When the lead goose become tired or confused they drop back into the formation and another goose takes the lead.

- Birds in the back of the formation honk encouragement to geese in front to maintain their position and speed.

- Geese have strong bonds and when one goose becomes sick or hurt, two geese drop back and stay with the goose until it is better or dies. Then they fly together to join another formation or until they reach the original group.

People can learn a lot from observing geese; working as a team increases productivity and discourages unproductive activities. Good teamwork provides an opportunity for individuals to take turns leading and feeling significant and empowered, and provides support and protection for team members when they are discouraged, weak, or make a mistake.

> No one can defeat us unless
> we defeat ourselves.
> —Dwight Eisenhower

Most teamwork literature suggests there is no "I" in team but this does not mean that individual effort is not needed or appreciated. On the contrary, personal effort is critical to the success of a team and good teams encourage individuals to be the best they can be while contributing to the overall mission of the organization in a collaborative manner so that all those involved are benefited.

There are a number of successful concepts that involve developing excellent teams and we will look at a few of these beginning with Zoglio (1993) who identified seven keys for a successful team; *commitment, contribution, communication, cooperation, conflict management, change management,* and *connections*. We'll examine each of these briefly:

- *Commitment.* Understanding the overall purpose of a group and committing to that purpose is a bonding experience that helps to ensure that the group stays focused and works collaboratively toward success. To ensure this commitment, each member of a group must have an opportunity have a part in the development of the overall purpose and the values that group members share. Each member must have opportunities to contribute to the goals of the group and to feel good about and recognized for their accomplishments.

> Teamwork is the ability to work together toward a common vision. The ability to direct individual accomplishments toward organizational objectives. It is the fuel that allows common people to attain uncommon results.
> —Andrew Carnegie

Family leaders should hold discussions from time to time to review the overall purpose and goals of a family, such as love, support and encouragement, making a difference in the lives of others, religion, academics, sports, or other areas that families agree are important.. Each member should have an opportunity to make contributions to the purpose and should be recognized for their part. Organizational members must also have an opportunity to contribute to the mission of the organization and they should feel a part of the organization and recognized appropriately for their involvement.

- *Contribution*. Each individual in a group must contribute something to the family or organization and each person will make different contributions at different levels. Family and organizational leaders need to be encouraging, supportive, and empowering in the development of different attributes that individual team members bring to the group. New and advanced skills and mutually beneficial attributes should be encouraged through a supportive environment. Team members are much more productive when they feel a part of the team; they gain confidence in their contributions and feel empowered.

Family and organizations can help group members to gain confidence by asking for individual input. Confidence will grow as individual ideas are included in team activities and when individuals are recognized for their part in helping the group be successful. Effective and appropriate education and training, appropriate resources, support, inclusion, and recognition lead to empowered and contributing team members.

- *Communication*. One of the most important criteria for successful teams is that encouragement to communicate often, openly, and effectively. The team environment must feel safe and encouraging for asking questions and making suggestions without the fear of feeling judged from a negative standpoint. Members must be able to make mistakes in communication without fearing reprisals or ridicule and be forgiven for mistakes when asked. A more open dialogue often leads to exciting and productive ideas and an enthusiastic team culture.

Communication can be more effective when team leaders encourage listening actively, being sensitive in the language used, offering and receiving feedback with consideration for other people, trusting and respecting the other person's position, and being as efficient with meeting times as possible. Interpersonal skills can be developed through educational training, seminars, workshops, counselors, or online resources, and should be considered when necessary.

> Never doubt that a small group of thoughtful, committed citizens can change the world; indeed, it is the only thing that ever has.
>
> —Margaret Mead

- *Cooperation.* Working well together is critical to the overall success of a team. The world can be very complicated and individuals need to share their information, concerns, and ideas in selfless manner for the overall good of the group. Steven Covey likes to use the term *interdependent* (Covey, 1989) because we are all truly interconnected and independence alone is an endangered term. Cooperation helps to build synergy, which leads to productivity, growth, and successful teams.

Smart leaders know how to encourage group members by serving as a role model for cooperation and by recognizing members for their cooperative efforts. They help ensure cooperation by demonstrating accurate and timely work, sharing progress notes with others, creating new ways to be successful, and by encouraging a healthy, open, trusting home or organizational atmosphere.

> Great discoveries and achievements invariably involve the cooperation of many minds.
>
> —Alexander Graham Bell

PART II   *Leading With Character, Purpose, & Passion at Work & at Home*

▸ *Conflict Management.* Having a difference of opinion on how best to use resources, on behavior, beliefs, religion, or a number of other areas is natural. Conflict that is managed effectively can stimulate creativity and lead to even more successful teams. When not managed well, issues can become more intense and future issues may not be addressed at all, which may lead to deception that add complications and tension among individuals.

Using effective models to manage conflict (see *Conflict Management* in the previous section) provides leaders in families and other groups with opportunities for individuals to work together to solve differences. Successful conflict management often leads to positive, shared solutions, making the group more effective and helping to develop trust and a stronger sense of camaraderie.

▸ *Change Management.* Change, like conflict, is inevitable. Families and organizations must be sensitive to changes ahead and evaluate the changes that are coming so they can decide which areas of their group processes, if any, need to adjust to be successful. Some things like group values or high quality associated with various activities may never change, but areas utilizing advanced technology and communication, for instance, may constantly need to be upgraded to assist the group in operating successfully.

Family and other group leaders must be alert to change and help group members focus on potential changes down the road so team members can work together in deciding what, if any, adjustments are needed to keep up with perceived and actual change. This requires a constant evaluation process by team members to determine if group change is necessary to meet changes in the world or to achieve a higher level of success.

> **You must be the change you wish to see in the world.**
> —Mahatma Gandhi

- *Connections.* Small groups invariably form in any family or organization for various reasons. Moms and dads form parental teams to discuss a child's development or ways to improve family communication. Organizational teams are formed to develop and promote specific products or to discuss ways to make the organization more financially solvent. Forming teams within a group is natural and often necessary. At the same time, it is important for leaders to monitor the progress of teams to make sure they connect with the overall purpose of the group and with the individuals the group is attempting to serve.

It is important that teams within an organization work parallel to the mission and that their work serves constituents. In a business, the constituents could be customers, clients, or patients. For families, it might be other family members such as grandparents, aunts, uncles, and cousins or individuals in the community. Making sure that teams serve constituents well and within the framework of the group's purpose is an important task for a leader. Recognizing group members who assist in that task is a significant key to success.

Another great concept to consider for effective team building was developed by Susan Heathfield in *Your Guide to Human Resources* (http://human resources.about.com/od/involvementteams/a/team_culture.htm). Heathfield states that it is important to foster a culture that is receptive for teamwork; a culture that encourages collaboration and where individuals share planning, decisions, and actions with each other.

She further explains that a culture like this can be created through the following actions:

- *Leaders communicate clearly that teamwork is expected.* Each person in a group must understand they are an integral part of a team and that they must work cooperatively for success to happen.

- *Leaders model teamwork through their work with others.* Unfortunately, for some leaders it's "do as I say, not as I do." Great leaders emulate the actions and values they expound.

- *Teamwork must be on record as being a significant part of team culture.* When values are discussed and listed within the group, teamwork should always be an integral part of the list.

- *Leaders reward and recognize responsible team members.* Team members who demonstrate collaboration receive higher recognition and rewards than those who try to go it alone.

- *Leaders provide consistent and effective communication relevant to teamwork.* Good leaders consistently provide information to team members regarding their collaborative efforts. This helps individuals focus on the great significance of teamwork.

Individuals working together effectively can accomplish so much more than people working separately. Not only are groups more successful working as a team, but individuals bond during teamwork activities and develop a more important feeling of belonging. It is a key responsibility of leaders in families and organizations to work tirelessly to bring individuals together as strong partners of a team.

> Coming together is a beginning,
> staying together is progress,
> working together is success.
>
> —Henry Ford

Reflection & Application

On a scale of 1 to 10 with 10 being the best, how would you rate the team-like qualities of the groups for which you are the leader or in which you are involved? What can you do to improve as a "team" leader?

_____
_____
_____
_____
_____
_____
_____
_____

Which of the concepts listed in the previous section could help your work group or family become an even stronger team?

_____
_____
_____
_____
_____
_____
_____

What concerted effort will you make to incorporate these ideas within your work group or family?

Embracing Diversity

According to some projections, by the year 2030 Asians, Hispanics, blacks and other minorities will make up about one-third of this country's population and senior citizens will make up a larger portion of the workforce then ever before because of the baby boom of 1946–1964. Additionally, thanks in large part to the Americans with Disabilities Act of 1990, disabled individuals are experiencing equal access and employment opportunities like never before. Our country's demographics are changing quickly and educational and business organizations are responding by requiring individuals to acquire knowledge and skills in cultural diversity (Allen, 2004).

Business operations have shifted to encompass a more global kind of economy. There is a huge diversity of customers, clients and suppliers in the marketplace (De Janasz, Dowd, and Schneider, 2002) and businesses must be prepared for this shift in paradigms. Educational institutions are constantly undergoing restructuring to receive and educate students from all corners of the world, and members of families must be well prepared for diversity in the workplace and in the community.

Regardless of differences in age, gender, nationality, race, ethnicity, religion, abilities, and other factors, group members share a number of similarities. They each feel the need to belong and to know that their membership in a group matters. This is as true for a family group as it is for all other groups. Our country and world are made up of individuals from all kinds of backgrounds; it is imperative, therefore, that leaders help group members gain knowledge, understanding, and acceptance about various differences in others so they can share positive experiences and be more effective in diverse situations. In a multi-cultural world, it is not only the practical approach but it is also the right thing to do.

> Diversity is the one true thing
> we all have in common.
> Celebrate it every day.
>
> —Anonymous

Unfortunately, there are a number of hurdles to understanding and accepting others that seem different. Many individuals around the globe grow up believing their culture is the best and all other cultures are inferior. This is called being *ethnocentric* and it is a condition that limits personal growth and effective interactions with others significantly. Others believe that individuals that share a certain trait, such as skin, hair, or eye color are all alike and this is referred to as *stereotyping*. Stereotyping is inaccurate and unfair, and also limits interpersonal communications and teamwork. Those who stereotype often go to the next level and pre-judge individuals based on the stereotype, a term referred to as being *prejudiced* and making a decision about someone before even meeting or interacting with them. And those who pre-judge others often *discriminate* toward those individuals, meaning they act in a certain way based on their prejudice which in turn was based on the stereotype.

These unfortunate mistakes have led to countless misunderstandings, disagreements, and conflicts. Dispelling these beliefs or helping to put them in proper perspective is therefore challenging but critical if groups are to work well together and succeed. And this is a challenge that family and organizational leaders have to address for the sake of all individuals involved in the group process.

> If we cannot end now our differences,
> at least we can make the world
> safe for diversity.
>
> —John F. Kennedy

There are a number of positions a leader can take to help his or her family or other groups embrace diversity effectively:

- *Awareness.* First, a leader needs to become aware of his or her culture and how that culture shapes the way life and people are perceived. It is important to recognize possible biases or stereotypes and to be able to deal with those biases effectively and fairly. A bias is an evaluation or an attitude, and attitudes are difficult to change but a leader must be open to positive change in order to share effective concepts for embracing diversity with other group members. Being aware of and respecting differences in others is also critical in the early stage of embracing diversity.

- *Provide Information on the Importance of Embracing Diversity.* A good leader should help others in the group become aware of their own possible biases and of the importance of diversity for practical and ethical reasons. Leaders should review some of the hurdles that exist on the way to effective cultural diversity; stereotyping, prejudices, and discrimination are examples. Becoming aware of one's own personal culture is critical; then, understanding the importance of valuing the culture of others is the next important step. A dialogue of ethical and practical reasons for embracing diversity must become part of the fabric of the group's formal and informal processes, and part of that discussion should include the importance of effectively embracing diversity in working toward the mission of the family or organization.

- *Empower Others through Training, Experiential Activities, and the Group Environment.* Training for effective cultural diversity can include classes, workshops, and experiential activities. Classroom and workshop activities can be initiated by connecting with local educational or religious institutions, checking with the local Chamber of Commerce, and an on-line search for experts in cultural diversity in your area. Classroom work must be followed up with activities in which individuals from different backgrounds work together to address simulated or real situations in a structured setting. Making the most of individual differences in solving problems helps to develop bonds and trust across diverse backgrounds. Along with these processes, family or organizational leaders must develop and promote a comfortable environment for all group members to share. This environment should include appropriate rewards for embracing diversity in working toward the group's mission.

> **Strength lies in differences, not in similarities.**
> —Stephen Covey

- *Serve as a Role Model.* For a leader to be successful in creating an effective culturally diverse group, then the leader must be perceived as a someone who embraces diversity for its many benefits and who discourages bias and unfairness. This will help tremendously in providing guidelines and encouragement for others and will set the stage for positive relationship building and greater successes overall.

- *Monitor Progress and make Adjustments if Necessary.* Like any significant part of a family or organization, the development of a successful culturally diverse group and environment must be monitored and adjusted if and when necessary. Informal or formal interviews, surveys, and focus-group meetings and observation can provide information on whether groups are headed in the right direction regarding embracing diversity.

Embracing diversity is the ethically right thing to do. Groups with individuals from different backgrounds and ideas can and do work together to complement each other's differences, leading to creative and synergistic efforts toward the group's mission. "If a group is unified, it is capitalizing on its diversity with everyone adding his or her perspective—way of thinking and way of acting—to each and every challenge faced by the group" (Weis & Gantt, 2004).

Reflection & Application

Do you have a good understanding of how important it is to develop groups that embrace different cultures? Explain why diversity is important to you and your groups.

_____
_____
_____
_____
_____
_____
_____
_____

What can you do to help your group become more competent in interactions with individuals from diverse backgrounds?

_____
_____
_____
_____
_____
_____
_____
_____

EPILOGUE

Families, businesses and other kinds of organizations deserve the very best leadership possible. If there was but one formula for effective leadership it would be documented in every book, journal, and magazine that dealt with the subject of leadership but there is not. No two concepts, leaders, or situations are exactly alike and it is important that leaders of various groups understand they must find their own paths through exploration, study, and experience to become the best leader possible. Leadership is about making a difference in situations and in lives, and good leaders are highly desired because it takes an enormous amount of talent and character to inspire and guide others effectively, consistently, and successfully.

We reaffirm our belief that *good leaders are made and not born*. If you want to make a difference and lead others in the quest for success, you must be willing and able to study, understand, and initiate ideas and concepts that can enable you to become a strong leader. *The Revised Integrated Leadership and Character Model* has leading with *character*, *purpose* and *passion* as its core and, therefore, using this model can result in leadership that is respected and trusted. Group members feel confident in leaders that have good character; they have a clearer and stronger focus when the purpose of the group is communicated effectively and prominently, and they can develop a stronger commitment to the purpose when passion is shared and encouraged. It is also important for leaders to possess or develop conceptual, technical, and human relationship skills or be able to collaborate with others who are competent in these areas because these areas are also critical to the success of most groups.

The *Revised Integrated Leadership and Character Model* can be an excellent concept in assessing and developing your own areas of strength, as well as in assessing and developing strengths in those around you. It has been presented to organizations nationally and internationally for use in the selection and training of staff members and can be equally helpful in the development of group members in other organizations and families. Incorporating the model in your leadership style may require a transformational commitment to change, and change often requires dogged determination on your part to make it happen and on the part of others to become receptive to change. But if it helps you in becoming the best leader possible, then it is worth every second of your time and of your effort. We wish you the very best on your journey!

BIBLIOGRAPHY

Allen, J. (2004). *Difference Matters: Communicating Social Identity.* Long Grove, IL: Waveland Press.

American Dietetic Association (2007). Safe and Healthy Diets. Path—*www.eatright.org.*

American Heart Association (2003). National Center: Dallas, TX.

Belasco, J.A., and Stayer, R.C. (1993). *Flight of the Buffalo.* New York: Warner.

Bennis, W., and Townsend, R. (1995). *Reinventing Leadership.* New York: Morrow Publishing.

Block, P. (1987). *The Empowered Manager: Positive Skills at Work.* San Francisco: Jossey-Bass Limited.

Bokeno, R.M., and Gantt, V. (2000). Dialogic mentoring: Core relationships for organizational learning. *Management Communication Quarterly* 14(2): 237–270.

Borisoff, D., and Victor, D. (1998). *Conflict Management: A Communication Skills Approach,* 2nd ed. Boston, MA: Allyn and Bacon.

Boverie, P., and Kroth, M. (March/April 2005). "Motivation: Nine ways to create a more passionate work environment—starting today!" Management File, Advancing Philanthropy (*www.afnet.org*).

Boverie, P., and Kroth, M. (2001). *Transforming Work: The Five Keys to Achieving Trust, Commitment, and Passion in the Workplace.* Cambridge, MA: Perseus Publishing.

Boylson, H.D. (1955). *Clara Barton: Founder of the American Red Cross.* New York: Random House.

Buber, M. (1970). *I and Thou.* New York: Charles Scribner's Sons.

Burns, J.M. (1978). *Leadership.* New York: Harper and Row.

Calumet (2003). Consistent Exercise and Sleep Routines. Path—*www.calumet.perdue.edu.*

Carnegie, D. (1885). *How to Enjoy Your Life and Your Job.* New York: Pocket Books.

Character Counts, (2007). The Six Pillars of Character. Path—*www. http://character counts.org/pdf/charactercounts_brochure.pdf.*

Covey, S. (1991) *Principle-Centered Leadership*. New York: Summit Books.

Covey, S. (1989). *The 7 Habits of Highly Effective People*. New York: Simon & Schuster.

Covey, S.R., Merrill, A.R., & Jones, D. (1998). *The Nature of Leadership*. Salt Lake City, Utah: Franklin Covey Company.

Depree, M. (1989). *Leadership Is an Art*. New York: Doubleday.

De Janasz, S., Dowd, K., and Schneider, B. (2002). *Interpersonal Skills in Organizations*. New York: McGraw Hill Publications.

De Vito, J. (2001). *The Interpersonal Communication Book*, 9th edition. New York: Harper Collins.

Edginton, C.R., and Ford, P.F. (1985). *Leadership in Recreation and Leisure Service Organizations*. New York: John Wiley and Sons.

Edginton, C.R., Hudson, S.D., and Ford, P. (1999). *Leadership in Recreation and Leisure Service Organizations*, 2nd edition. Champaign, IL: Sagamore Publishing.

Eisenberg, E.M., and Goodall, Jr., H.L. (2004). *Organizational Communication*, 4th edition. Boston/New York: Bedford/St. Martin.

Eisler, R. (1995). *Sacred Pleasure*. New York: Harper Collins.

English, F.W. (1992). *Educational Administration: The Human Science*. New York: Harper Collins.

Food and Nutrition Information Center (2005). Healthy Diets. Path—*www.nal.usda.gov/fnic*.

French, Jr., J.P.P., and Raven, B. (1959). The Basis of Social Power. In D. Cartwright (ed.), *Studies in Social Power*. Ann Arbor, MI: Institute for Social Research.

Fromm, E. (1956). *The Art of Loving: An Inquiry into the Nature of Love*. New York: Harper and Row.

Gantt, V. (1997). Beneficial mentoring is for everyone: a reaction paper. Paper presented at the National Communication Association Convention, Chicago.

Gelb, M. (1998). *How to Think Like Leonardo da Vinci*. New York: Dell Publishing.

Greenleaf, R.K. (1996). The Strategies of a Leader. In D.M. Frick and L.C. Spears (eds.), *Focus on Leadership: Servant-leadership for the 21st Century* New York: John Wiley and Sons (pp. 19–25).

Greenleaf, R.K. (1970). *The Servant Leader*. Indianapolis: The Robert Greenleaf Center.

Hardy, J. (1984). *Managing for Impact in Nonprofit Organizations*. Erwin, TN: Essex Press.

Harrison, E.F. (1983). *Management and Organizations*. Boston: Houghton Mifflin.

Hersey, P., and Blanchord, K. (1977). *Management of Organizational Behavior—Utilizing Human Resources*, 3rd ed. Englewood Cliffs, NJ: Prentice-Hall.

Hesse, H. (1956). *Journey to the East*. New York: Noonday Press/Farrar Straus and Giroux.

Hitt, W.D. (1988). *The Leader Manager: Guidelines for Action*. Columbus, OH: Battelle Press.

Holander, E.P. (1978). What Is the Crisis of leadership? *Humanitas*, 14(3), 285–296.

Holy Bible, KJV (1970). Camden, NJ: Thomas Nelson, Inc.

Homans, G.C. (1950). *The Human Group*. New York: Harcourt, Brace and World.

House, R., Hanges, P. Javidan, J., Dorfman, P., and Gupta, V. (eds.) (2004). *Culture, Leadership, and Organizations: The GLOBE Study of 62 Societies*. Thousand Oaks, CA: Sage Publications.

Healthfield, S. (2007). Your Guide to Human Resources Path—http://human resources.about.com/od/involvementteams/a/team_culture.htm

Hunter, J.C. (1998). *The Servant: The Simple Story about the True Essence of Leadership*. New York: Crown Publishing Group.

Ivancevich, J., and Matteson, M. (1980). *Stress and Work. A Managerial Perspective*. Glenview, IL: Scott Foresman.

Jackson, M., White, L., and Herman, M. (1997). *Mission Accomplished: The Workbook*. Washington, DC: Nonprofit Risk Management Center.

Jinkins, M., and Jinkins, D.B. (1998). *The Character of Leadership: Political Realism and Public Virtue in Nonprofit Organizations*. San Francisco: Jossey-Bass, Inc.

Katz, D., Maccoby, N., and Morse, N.C. (1950). *Productivity, Supervision and Morale in an Office Situation*. Ann Arbor: Survey Research Center, University of Michigan.

Katz, R.L. (1995). *Skills of an Effective Administrator*. Harvard Business Review, 33(1), 33–42.

Kelly, M. (2005). *The Seven Levels of Intimacy: The Art of Loving and the Joy of Being Loved*. New York: Beacon Publishing.

Kelly, M. (2004). *The Rhythm of Live: Living Every Day with Passion & Purpose*. New York: Beacon Publishing.

Koch, A., and Peden, P. (1993). *The Live and Selected Writings of Thomas Jefferson*. New York: Random House.

Kotter, J.P. (May–June 1990). What Leaders Really Do. *Harvard Business Review*, Volume 68 (3), 103–111.

Kouzes, J., and Poser, B. (2002). *The Leadership Challenge*. San Francisco: John Wiley and Sons, Inc.

Levy, J.E. (1975). *Cesar Chavez: Autobiography of La Causa.* New York: W.W. Norton.
Loeb, P.R. (2004). *The Impossible Will Take a Little Time.* New York: Perseus Books Group.
Luthans, F. (1967). *The Human Organization.* New York: McGraw-Hill.
MacIntyre, A.C. (1981). *After Virtue.* Notre Dame, IN: University of Notre Dame Press.
Maslow, A.H. (1954). *Motivation and Personality.* New York: Harper and Row.
Maslow, A.H. (1943). A Theory of Human Motivation. *Psychological Review,* Vol. 50, 370–96.
Maxwell, J. (2004). *Today Matters: 12 Daily Practices to Guarantee Tomorrow's Success.* New York: Time Warner Book Group.
Maxwell, J. (1999). *The 21 Indispensable Qualities of a Leader: Becoming the Person Others Will Want to Follow.* Nashville, TN: Thomas Nelson Publications.
Maxwell, J. (1993) *Developing the Leader Within You.* Nashville, TN: Thomas Nelson, Publications.
Northouse, P.G. (2007). *Leadership: Theory and Practice,* 4th ed. Thousand Oaks, CA: Sage Publications, Inc.
Peters, T.J., and Waterman, R.H. (1982). *In Search of Excellence.* New York: Harper and Row.
Petry, A. (1955). *Harriett Tubman.* New York: Thomas Y. Crowell Company.
Purkey, W.W., and Siegel, B. (2003). *Becoming an Invitational Leader: A New Approach to Professional and Personal Successes.* Atlanta: Humanics Trade Group Publication.
Raffoni, M. (2006). *Are You Spending Your Time the Right Way?* Boston: Harvard Business School Publishing Co.
Reddin, W.H.J. (1970). *Managerial Effectiveness.* New York: McGraw-Hill.
Seven Keys to Healthy Relationships (2004). Path—*http://www.relationship-helps-and-advice.com/healthyrelationships.html*
Richards, N. (1968). *People of Destiny, Helen Keller.* Chicago: Children's Press.
Rost, J.C. (1993). *Leadership for the Twenty-first Century.* Westport, CT: Praeger.
Senge (1990). *The Fifth Discipline: The Art and Practice of the Learning Organization.* New York: Doubleday Publishing Co.
Sims, R.R., and Quatro, S.A. (eds.) (2005). *Leadership: Succeeding in the Private, Public, and Not-for-Profit Sectors.* Armonk, NY: M.E. Sharpe, Inc.
Stogdill, R. (1974). *Handbook of Leadership: A Survey of Theory and Research.* New York: Macmillan Company.

Stodgill, R., and Coons, A. (1975). *Leader Behavior's Description and Measurement.* Columbus: Bureau of Business Research, Ohio State University.

Tolle, E. (1997). *The Power of NOW: A Guide to Spiritual Enlightenment.* Novato, CA: New World Library.

Utley, R.M. (1988). *Cavalier in Buckskin.* Norman: University of Oklahoma Press.

Van der Smissen, B. (1990). *Legal Liability and Risk Management for Public and Private Entities* (Vol. 2). Cincinnati, OH.

Vroom, V.H., and Yetton, P.W. (1973). *Leadership and Decision Making.* Pittsburgh: University of Pittsburg Press, 1973.

Weis, R. (1998). *Service Learning Training Manual for Faculty K–16.* Murray, KY: American Humanics, Murray State University.

Weis, R., and Gantt, V. (2004). *Knowledge and Skill Development in Nonprofit Organizations.* Peosta, IA: Eddie Bowers Publishing Company.

Weis, R., and Gantt, V. (2002). *Leadership and Program Development in Nonprofit Organizations.* Peosta, IA: Eddie Bowers Publishing Company.

Weis, R., Rogers, K., and Broughton, J. (2004) Selecting and Training Staff and Volunteer Members for Leadership, Character, and Competencies. *The Journal of Volunteer Administration*, Vol. 22, No. 1, pp. 38–41

Wellness in Your Life (2005). South Deerfield, MA: Channing Bete Company.

Wolf, T. (1991). *Managing a Nonprofit Organization.* New York: Prentice Hall.

Wren, J.T. (1995). *The Leader's Companion.* New York: The Free Press.

Zoglio, S. (1993). Seven Keys to Building Great Workteams. Available on-line. Path—*http//www.teambuildinginc.com* (select: "Articles"; scroll down and select: "7 Keys to Building Great Workteams").

ABOUT THE AUTHORS

Roger M. Weis, Ed.D. is Campus Director and Professor for the American Humanics/Youth and Nonprofit Leadership (AH/YNL) program at Murray State University (MSU). He has twice been selected as student advisor of the year and was the first recipient of the American Humanics National Award for Excellence in Leadership and the first recipient of the Distinguished Service Learning and Civic Engagement Award at MSU. During his tenure, the AH/YNL program at MSU has received numerous national and local awards for excellence in academics, leadership, service, and research and has been the largest program in the country for quite some time.

Dr. Weis has also served as chair of the American Humanics Directors Association for two terms and on the AH National Board of Directors for two terms. He is the founding chair of the Big Brothers/Big Sisters program in Murray, the Campus Connection Volunteer Center and the MSU Center for Service Learning and Civic Engagement, and the founding co-chair of the Service Learning Scholars program and the Health Matters for Students program. Previously, he has had four books published, three of which are textbooks dealing in part with leadership. He has presented leadership workshops and forums to youth, human service, and other organizations and has lectured and made presentations to over 100 institutions of education around the world including Oxford and Cambridge Universities in England and Trinity College in Ireland.

Vernon W. Gantt, Ph.D. is Professor Emeritus of Organization Communication from Murray State University where he served as professor and chair of the department. Having taught at MSU for 27 years prior to retirement in 2000, he has received the Murray State University Alumni Association's Distinguished Professor Award, the Kentucky Communication Association's Lifetime Service to the Profession Award, and the Kentucky Communication Association's Presidential Award for Teaching. He remains a busy consultant and author having published two textbooks on leadership and other aspects of the nonprofit field. He has been chair of the American Humanics Advisory Council at MSU for 20 years and a Trustee for the National American Humanics program for the same time period. He is a leader for Rotary International and has served as a consultant/volunteer for the organization as well as for Boy Scouts of America, the American Red Cross, American Cancer Society, and his church.

His consulting list includes state and local government agencies, national and international professional associations, Ingersoll-Rand, Briggs and Stratton, AE Staley, Tennessee Valley Authority, and General Tire. He is also an experienced mediator and works as a trainer for Court Appointed Special Advocates (CASA).

LEADERSHIP DEVELOPMENT WORKSHOPS AND SEMINARS

You can make a major difference in the way you and others in your business, organization, or group lead by requesting a workshop or seminar from the authors of *Leading With Character, Purpose & Passion!*

We offer half-day and full-day interactive workshops and informative seminars for groups in this country and abroad. If you'd like to know more about the workshops or seminars, contact: *roger.weis@murraystate.edu* or call Dr. Roger Weis at 270-809-3808.

Workshops and seminars concentrate on individual leadership development for each member of your group.

A percentage of all profits from workshops and seminars are donated to charitable organizations.